Training in Practice

Steve Truelove

Copyright © Steve Truelove, 1997

The right of Steve Truelove to be identified as author of this work has been asserted in accordance with the Copyright, Designs and Patents Act 1988.

First published 1997

2 4 6 8 10 9 7 5 3 1

Blackwell Publishers Ltd
108 Cowley Road
Oxford OX4 1JF
UK

Blackwell Publishers Inc
Commerce Place
350 Main Street
Maldon MA 02148

British Library Cataloguing in Publication Data
A CIP catalogue record for this book is available from the British Library.

Library of Congress Cataloging-in-Publication Data

Truelove, Steve.
  Training in practice / Steve Truelove.
      p.   cm.
  Includes bibliographical references and index.
  ISBN 0-631-20251-X (alk. paper)
    1. Employees——Training of——Methodology.   I. Title.
HF5549.5.T7T78   1997   96-40884
658.3'124—dc21   CIP
ISBN 0-631-20251-X
Typeset in 11 on 13 pt Bookman
by Intype London Ltd
Printed in Great Britain by Hartnolls Ltd., Bodmin, Cornwall

This book is printed on acid-free paper

Contents

List of Examples

Preface

This book has been written in response to the introduction of the Certificate in Training Practice by the Institute of Personnel and Development. This new qualification is very much aimed at practitioners, and my publishers, Blackwells, suggested that I might produce a suitable text to accompany the course. When reviewing the textbooks already available, it seemed to me that many of them were rather heavy and academic in nature. Although some training textbooks are available which are very accessible, they tend to be single topic books dealing with only part of the role of the trainer.

Whilst considering whether or not to write this text, I was asked by a young woman who was newly appointed to the role of trainer if I were to recommend just one book which she should buy, which it should be. As I couldn't do so, my aim with this text is that it should be regarded as particularly suitable for the new trainer and will be recommended as such by others. Or at least by me.

In order to facilitate its use as a set book for courses such as the Certificate in Training Practice, I have included a number of activities at the end of each section which I hope will be found helpful. The reader who is not following such a programme may, of course, need to adapt the methodology for personal use.

Although there are some references to theories and models in this text, there are not very many. When I have given a theoretical model, I have usually given only one rather than discuss a range of possibilities. I believe that for many new trainers the degree of academic discussion about what is essentially a practical profession can be daunting and even alienating. However, there is a wealth of knowledge available in books, and for those who wish to do so I have tried to provide a reading list of genuinely useful books. I have not tried to list every book I have ever heard of, and there are many good books available which are not included in this list.

This book contains few, if any, new ideas. It does not seek to break new ground but rather to collate existing knowledge in a succinct and accessible way. It is not intended to cover all aspects of training and training management, concentrating instead on the core techniques which the practitioner must master. It is not intended, either, for the strategic thinker or policymaker who is concerned with long-term organizational improvement.

The influence of a myriad previous writers is readily acknowledged. Special thanks to Sylvia Downs for her approval of the short passage on MUD in chapter 2.

Steve Truelove

1

■

Identifying Training Needs

Everybody is ignorant, only on different subjects.
Will Rogers, Chambers Book of Quotations

Overview

Before considering what techniques for identifying learning needs are available to us, it may be useful to clarify one or two concepts. First, let us look at a definition of the term 'training need':

> The difference between actual and required human performance at work forms the basis of the need. (A. H. Anderson, 1993)

This neatly sums up the concept. Other writers use terms such as 'performance gap' to convey the same concept. And it is in the sensitivity of this concept that our first difficulty lies. Remember that you are dealing with people, and that these gaps may be sources of embarrassment, the beginnings of disciplinary proceedings or the causes of deep-seated resentments for some people. It is all too easy to go blundering about, enthusiastically determining training needs with insufficient regard to the feelings of the individuals involved. Attempts to soften this by using language such as 'not yet competent' can never be wholly successful.

The second difficulty is that a training need is only one of several possible causes of the performance gap. Include the other possible causes and the list becomes:

- poor resources
- lack of ability
- lack of motivation
- training need

It is not always easy to determine the reason, or reasons, underlying poor performance. Many people find it easiest to blame others, or to blame poor resources. Of course, sometimes they are right to do so. Investigation is needed to determine where the root of the performance gap lies. There may be more than one of these factors involved.

POOR RESOURCES

Although it is often said that 'a bad workman blames his tools', it is equally true that someone who is provided with inadequate or inappropriate tools may perform below the level which he or she is capable of. For example, you might investigate the poor performance of someone employed as a cleaner, and find that he or she was struggling to use a worn-out and inefficient vacuum cleaner. It would, perhaps, lead you to conclude that it would be more sensible to invest in a new vacuum cleaner than in sending the person concerned on a training course.

Another resource limitation that is often blamed for poor performance is that of time. Again, it may be difficult to ascertain whether this is an excuse, or genuine. It will be necessary to compare the performance of different people doing the same job with the same constraints in order to decide this. In many instances, you will have to rely on the judgement of others if you do not have the technical expertise to make the analysis for yourself.

LACK OF ABILITY

This refers to the individual's innate abilities, over which they have no influence. Limitations in intelligence levels, aptitude for learning, manual dexterity or a range of other abilities can inhibit job performance. If this is the case, it may indicate that poor selection procedures have resulted in people being appointed to jobs for which they are not suited. Often, though, it is indicative of changes that have occurred in the job that the jobholder is now struggling, whereas he or she could once cope. For example, many manual workers now have to deal with new technology which requires a different set of abilities from those previously needed, and many people who were recruited for technical jobs now have to deal directly with customers.

We are not all equally capable of learning new things. Mathematical ability, problem solving, visual acuity, and so on, vary widely between individuals. Training may not produce any improvement.

LACK OF MOTIVATION

Motivation is a complex subject. Poor motivation may be due to many things – boredom, lack of challenge, a feeling of being unappreciated, resentment for some past wrong. Some people are much easier to motivate than others. The key question is whether or not the individual's motivation appears to have varied. Someone who was once highly motivated, and who is now indifferent, may be sending out strong signals: 'Something is wrong. I am not happy.'

It may not be easy to get to the bottom of the problem, nor is a solution always possible, but attempting to cure a motivational problem by inappropriate means may make matters worse. However, some training solutions may be highly motivational. Training gives people attention, which can be motivating. It should stimulate them with new ideas, which can provide a fresh look at an old job.

It can also put them in contact with other people whose enthusiasm may prove to be infectious.

TRAINING NEED

The final reason for poor performance is lack of competence. That is to say, lack of knowledge or skills in someone who has the ability to acquire that knowledge or skill. In other words, a training need. This may, in turn, be linked to poor motivation or it may be due to lack of opportunity. Competence comes through learning. Learning comes either through experience, training, or through a combination of the two. However, trying to address a performance problem through training when it is really due to a lack of innate ability will not work.

At this point I think it is helpful to introduce a simple framework for understanding training needs. That produced by Tom Boydell in 1976 distinguishes between three types of need.

* Organizational training needs
* Occupational training needs
* Individual training needs

ORGANIZATIONAL TRAINING NEEDS

An organizational training need is one that applies to the whole organization. There are two main sub-categories.

1 *Training needs which are generated by change* – changes such as:

* new products are being made or sold
* new technology has been introduced
* new legislation affects the organization
* new managerial systems (e.g. total quality management) are being introduced
* the ownership of the organization has changed
* there have been acquisitions, mergers, disposals, or other structural changes

2 *Training needs which must be met to produce change*
  – changes to situations such as:

  - productivity is too low
  - morale is very low
  - the corporate culture is inhibiting development
  - people are not customer-focused

OCCUPATIONAL TRAINING NEEDS

An occupational training need is one that applies to a particular category of employee. It may be a consequence of a wider organizational change, or it may have arisen for one group of workers in isolation. Again, we can distinguish two main sub-categories.

1 *Training needs which are generated by change* –
  changes such as:

  - there is a new software package for accounts
  - there is a tighter system for access to the building to be operated by the security officers
  - personnel officers and training officers are to be merged into new roles as human resources consultants

2 *Training needs which must be met to produce change*
  – changes to situations such as:

  - security officers are rather grumpy with visitors
  - senior managers are still using gender-specific terms when referring to jobs
  - middle managers are poor at solving problems
  - higher output is required from production
  - the fitters take a long time when repairing machines

INDIVIDUAL TRAINING NEEDS

An individual training need may be thought of as an occupational need that applies only to a specific individual as opposed to the whole category of employees.

1 *Training needs which are generated by change* – change such as:

- one of the production crew is now responsible for completing production records
- Mark is going to be visiting the Madrid office quite frequently and will need to learn Spanish
- Jill has been asked to prepare a detailed training budget for the first time

2 *Training needs which must be met to produce change* – situations such as:

- if Kate could operate the switchboard then Mary could spend longer on the graphic design and we wouldn't need to use an agency
- if Martin could do some interviewing then Sue could become more involved in training
- if Paula could learn to speak Italian we wouldn't need an agent over there
- Richard must start selling more

MAINTENANCE AND DEVELOPMENT NEEDS

Another way of thinking about training needs is to divide them into maintenance and development needs.

Maintenance needs are those training needs that must be met in order for the organization, occupational grouping or individual to maintain current performance. This can include training in order to keep the numbers up. For example, an insurance intermediary may employ 100 telesales staff. If 15 per cent of them leave or transfer each year, then 15 replacements will need to be trained. 'Maintenance training' also refers to the process of ensuring that performance does not deteriorate through sloppy practice or lack of feedback. Just as professional soldiers and top sportsmen and sportswomen train regularly to maintain skills, some workplace skills need to be refreshed from time to time.

Development needs are those concerned with the promotion of new learning, taking an individual, an occupation or even the whole organization into new learning arenas.

Both types of need are equally important.

A final way of distinguishing types of need is to consider proactive and reactive training. Proactive identification of needs is concerned with anticipating needs before they arise; reactive identification is responding to problems after they have arisen. The way in which the concepts of maintenance/development and reactive/proactive interact is shown in example 1.1.

	Maintenance	Development
Reactive	Correcting job performance failures	Helping people cope with new work
Proactive	Avoiding job performance failures	Helping people to prepare for future roles

Example 1.1 Interaction of concepts of training needs

It is tempting to regard being proactive as good, and being reactive as bad. In fact, a balance needs to be struck. Organizations change so rapidly that not all needs may be anticipated, and the trainer must have a willingness and capacity to respond to line managers' urgent requests as they arise. If, however, no proactive identification takes place, the trainer will be constantly firefighting and will have little opportunity to plan sensibly for the future.

Now that we have introduced various ways of thinking about training needs, we will proceed to consider techniques to help identify them. The identification of broad, strategic, organizational needs is outside the scope of this book and the reader should refer to the texts listed at the end of this section. The techniques given below are straightforward and can be readily used when looking at occupational and individual needs.

Job and Task Analysis

There are many reasons for analysing jobs and tasks. One common reason is to provide a basis for job evaluation, another is to be precise about requirements in a selection situation. There are also many different systems of analysis. Some seem to generate a multitude of documents, others use highly involved and sophisticated methodology. In their book *Job Analysis*, Pearn and Kandola (1988) describe 18 different analytical techniques. The process described below is a simple and traditional approach.

BACKGROUND

An analogy of digging a hole can well be applied to the task of job analysis. Both the area to be covered and the depth are arrived at by knowing the purpose of the hole. This analogy goes further in that the task can be both tedious and messy. The area of a particular job to be analysed and the depth are arrived at by knowing the purpose of the analysis exercise. (Malcolm Craig, in Truelove (ed.), 1995)

JOB ANALYSIS

I am using the term 'job analysis' to describe the level of analysis which takes us to the stage of writing a job description. This is a collection of statements regarding the functions performed in a job grouped in a way which helps a reader to get 'the big picture' of what is involved. The following are the most widely used methods of gathering information to prepare a job description.

• Interviewing the jobholder(s)
• Interviewing the boss of the jobholder

- Direct observation
- Asking the jobholder to keep a record of what is done (time sheet or diary)

Whichever method or combination of methods is used, the aim is to provide a descriptive document which clarifies understanding of the functions performed in the job. To aid understanding further, certain key facts are usually inserted at the front of the description. The format and contents of the front section will vary from one organization to another, but typically may comprise the following.

Job title   The official title as noted on personnel records. Take care to avoid any terms which imply sex discrimination (e.g. tealady, repairman).

Reports to · The position which has line responsibility for the job being described.

Responsible for   A list of any subordinates.

Purpose   A short, often single-sentence, description of the main objective of the job.

Location   Relevant information regarding site or department.

General   Any other relevant information.
Other commonly included pieces of information relate to pay grade, hours of work and working conditions. These are not particularly useful from the trainer's viewpoint, but may be required for other purposes.
The job description then proceeds to list what is done in the job. There is some confusion in the terminology used in job analysis. I find the use of the term 'responsibility' unhelpful, and prefer to use the term 'duty' for a chunk of work described at this level. Later on, a duty may be broken down into smaller 'tasks'. Note that in

the (very simple) example given in example 1.2 several activities have been clustered together under relevant headings. Each of these duties starts with a word ending with an 'ing'. The key to describing what is done in the duty is to start each sentence with an active verb – 'answers, places, assists', etc.

Once a job description has been completed, we can then proceed to analyse the components of the job

---

Job Description – Telephonist

Reports to: The administration manager
Responsible for: No subordinates
Purpose: To provide a prompt, efficient and
                         courteous telephone service for a regional
                         operating centre
Location: Main Building, Northern ROC
General: The postholder is one of two operating a
                         modern switchboard serving 340
                         extensions
Duties:

Receiving calls
Answers incoming calls promptly and courteously. Ascertains the nature of the call and directs it to the most appropriate person. Takes messages accurately when required.

Outgoing calls
Places calls for senior staff and may assist other staff with difficult or overseas calls

Dealing with emergencies
Implements set procedures to deal with fire or other incidents

Operating fax machine
Sends and receives messages by fax

Other duties
Assists with various office duties from time to time, including covering on reception

---

Example 1.2 A simple job description

further. This is done by clarifying in more detail the stages involved in each operation through task analysis.

TASK ANALYSIS

Many training situations do not require the in-depth breakdown of tasks into small component parts. However, some complex tasks need to be painstakingly analysed in order that an accurate and detailed picture is created which will form the basis of a training manual or programme. One of the consequences of the widespread use of information technology is that many people must learn to find their way around software packages. These are becoming increasingly large and versatile, and while some people cope well by trial and error and by using the manual, many others get stuck and give up. Even those who cope well may remain ignorant of some of the facilities available to them in the software, or may have found a laborious way to accomplish a task that has a much quicker solution available. The purpose of structured training is to ensure everyone learns the most effective methods of performing the required tasks, and learns them faster than by trial and error.

The process of analysis is one of breaking down operations into component parts. How small these component parts should be is a matter of judgement which should take account of the existing knowledge of the learner. Will he or she already know the procedure for 'Open File Manager'? If so, it would be a waste of time analysing that operation further. On the other hand, if the learner does not know what is meant, then right at the beginning of the training you will have needlessly created a feeling of inadequacy and confusion. It is usually best to analyse in full detail and skip unnecessary explanation at the time of training if it is clearly not required. The analytical process itself is good preparation for instruction: it makes sure you know all there is to know before you start trying to teach someone else.

To continue with the example already given for a

telephonist: the duty of 'sends messages by fax' could end up as:

1 loads document
2 dials number of destination
3 returns document and confirmation of transmission to
  originator

and so on. This depth of analysis may be adequate for training purposes. That is, to act as a sequential series of prompts for a competent person to use in the instruction of someone else. If more depth is required, the analysis may be more detailed.

1 Loading documents

1.1 Place the document face down on the tray
1.2 Adjust the document guide to match the width of
    the document
1.3 Slide the guide to ensure that the document is
    centred on the feeder
1.4 Gently insert the leading edge of the document
    into the loading slot until you hear a beep
1.5 Select desired resolution

and so on.

Even now, more detail may be required. In the above example, 1.5 might be expanded.

1.5 Select desired resolution

1.5.1 Press TX.MODE to cycle through FINE, SUPER
      FINE, or STANDARD modes
1.5.2 Press PHOTO if sending photographs

and so on.

It can also be appreciated that the above, although giving a sequence of operations, does not give the trainee any information as to when it is appropriate to use different modes or the consequences of each action (e.g. 'fine or super-fine modes are slower and therefore more costly').

Often extra information is useful. There are many

approaches to presenting the information from task analysis. One is to use the four headings shown in example 1.3. Another way is to incorporate all the information into discrete steps.

1 Select 'Create New Chart' from the main menu
2 Select 'From Gallery' from the Create New Chart menu to display the Chart Gallery
3 Select the chart type by pressing the number in the upper left . . .

and so on.

> Always remember to include any necessary information regarding safety, whatever format is used. If you fail to do so and someone is injured following your instructions, you could be liable for prosecution.

FAULTS ANALYSIS

The key skill in many jobs is recognizing when something has gone wrong and knowing what to do to put things right. Fault-finding procedures can be analysed systematically and a faults analysis chart produced (example 1.4). Good examples of these can be found in popular car manuals.

SKILLS ANALYSIS

Once the task breakdown has been completed to the required depth, each operation may be examined to determine what skills or background knowledge are necessary for its successful completion. In the examples given under the heading 'Task analysis' above, the operations are mainly procedural and do not require particular skills or knowledge. However, if we look at an aspect of the job of the telephonist such as 'Receiving calls' this could be considered to require a number of skills and considerable knowledge (see example 1.5).

When completed for all tasks, this stage is sometimes

What is done?	How is it done?	Points to ensure	Extra information
List the stages in a task starting each one with an active verb	Describe briefly how the operation is performed	Register factors that will affect performance	Note any other information which may be helpful or necessary
		List pointers that will show the trainee whether the operation is proceeding correctly Use sensory words like 'see' or 'feel' to describe signals which must be recognized	
Set up directory defaults	Select 'Setup' from the main menu	Save any work in progress before commencing	Using the arrow keys and pressing 'Enter' or by using the mouse and clicking on either button
	Select 'Defaults'	The Default Settings screen should now appear	
	Press Tab Type 'C:\' and the name of the directory containing your spreadsheet files		

Example 1.3 Task analysis

Fault	Causes	Remedies
File name invalid	Space, comma, or other character used	Remove the character and replace by letter or number
	More than eight characters	Rename with eight or fewer characters

Example 1.4 Faults analysis

Task	Knowledge	Skill
Answers incoming calls promptly and courteously	Company procedure for greeting callers	Switchboard operation
		Assertive and courteous telephone manner
Ascertains the nature of the call and directs it to the most appropriate person	Functions within the company	Questioning and listening techniques
	Extensions	
Takes messages accurately when required	Company procedure for recording messages	Judging when to offer to take messages
		Memo-writing proficiency

Example 1.5 Knowledge and skill breakdown

referred to as a 'job specification'. It may form the basis for the design of a training programme (see chapter 2). Otherwise, the completed task analysis or job specification may be used as a yardstick against which to assess current performance. If someone cannot do all the required tasks, then a training need is indicated. This approach has been developed extensively in the UK in the National Vocational Qualification system.

Skill Matrices

A quick and effective way of identifying training needs at an occupational level is to construct a skill matrix. For example, if we were to look at a workshop involved in the modification of light vans for a specialist purpose, we might arrive at a list of operations (perhaps at the 'duty' level).

- Cut off roof
- Cut out windows
- Cut out vents
- Fit high roof
- Fit windows
- Fit vents
- Fit panelling
- Thread wiring

We might have nine employees in this workshop and be able to ascertain whether or not each one is capable of doing each operation. A matrix may now be constructed (example 1.6). From this matrix it can readily be seen that we have some possible problem areas.

Name	Cut off roof	Cut out windows	Cut out vents	Fit high roof	Fit windows	Fit vents	Fit panelling	Thread wiring
R. Amos	√	√	√	√	√	√	√	
B. Borg				√		√		√
D. Cox							√	
H. Dawes	√	√	√					
M. Earl								√
F. Fry				√				
G. Grant						√	√	
S. Hunt			√	√		√	√	
J. Joyce							√	

Example 1.6 Skill matrix

One problem might be that there are many operations which can only be performed by two people. The line manager may or may not be aware of this picture. Often the problem will be overlooked until, say, Dawes goes sick while Amos is on leave. On the other hand, this may not be an issue if 'roof cutting' is a once-a-month job and we can always get a subcontractor to do it if stuck.

Another problem could be that Cox, Earl, Fry and Joyce can each only perform one operation. Again this may or may not be a problem. Perhaps they are all new to the job, or perhaps have some limitation which stops them learning other operations. The reasons must be investigated. If there is not an acceptable reason, then what should the desired skill situation be? If we discuss the matter with line management, they might say: 'We want everyone to be able to do at least three operations. We want at least three people capable of doing each cutting operation, and four people capable of doing each of the other operations.'

Our matrix can now be amended as shown in example 1.7.

We are now in a position to discuss how the various gaps should be addressed and develop a training plan

Name	Cut off roof	Cut out windows	Cut out vents	Fit high roof	Fit windows	Fit vents	Fit panelling	Thread wiring	Total	Need	Gap
R. Amos	√	√	√	√	√	√	√		7	3	-
B. Borg					√	√		√	3	3	-
D. Cox							√		1	3	2
H. Dawes	√	√	√						3	3	-
M. Earl								√	1	3	2
F. Fry					√				1	3	2
G. Grant						√	√		2	3	1
S. Hunt				√	√	√	√		4	3	-
J. Joyce							√		1	3	2
Total	2	2	2	2	4	4	5	2			
Need	3	3	3	4	4	4	4	4			
Gap	1	1	1	2	-	-	-	2			

Example 1.7 Skill matrix with gap indications

accordingly. However, so far we have only considered the question 'Can he or she perform the operation?' and have answered that question by using a tick or not – in other words, giving a yes or no answer. Often, the position is more complex. Grant *can* do wire threading, but is very slow. Borg *can* fit panelling, but the quality of her work is not up to standard. A variety of ways of adding detail to the picture are possible! In example 1.8, grades (A, B, 1, 2) are given.

Name	Cut off roof	Cut out windows	Cut out vents	Fit high roof	Fit windows	Fit vents	Fit panelling	Thread wiring
R. Amos	A1	A1	A1	A2	A1	A1	A1	B2
B. Borg					B1	A2		A1
D. Cox							B2	
H. Dawes	A1	A1	A1	B2	B2	B2		
M. Earl								A1
F. Fry		B2			A1			B2
G. Grant						A1	A1	
S. Hunt		B1		A1	A1	A2	A1	
J. Joyce							A1	B2

Key:
A – Quality to standard required
B – Quality below standard required
1 – Speed to required standard
2 – Speed below required standard

Example 1.8 Skill matrix showing gradations of competence

A more complex picture has now emerged. Other coding possibilities include the use of percentages to indicate speed, or more sophisticated definitions of competence such as:

A = fully competent, including fault rectification
B = fully competent for straightforward operations
C = competent to deal with straightforward operations with assistance
D = competent to assist others
E = not yet competent

One retail organization I know of developed a system

whereby competence was denoted by the use of red, silver and gold stars. This positive and motivating approach was made 'user friendly' by the skill matrix being displayed in the staff room at each branch. Not only were the training needs easily determined by the line manager, but achieving competence was rewarded by a certification system which was in turn linked to pay.

Interviewing

Interviewing is a technique that can appear to be very simple when used by an experienced practitioner. Although some people are naturally better at interviewing, the key skills of a good investigative interviewer are all capable of being learned. The first two skills are common to all types of interview – questioning and listening.

QUESTIONING AND LISTENING

These two investigative skills are inseparable; one supports and reinforces the other. For trainers these skills are crucial not only at the stage of identifying training needs, but also during instruction and evaluation. Many trainers who recognize that the ability to talk well is vital often underestimate the importance of questioning and listening. Hearing, which is an ability which may be difficult to improve, is not the same as listening which is a skill which can be significantly enhanced by training. Questioning is something that everyone can do but which some people learn to do much more effectively than others.

In an interview to determine training needs, the interviewer may be delving into very emotive and sensitive areas. To ensure that the interviewee feels comfortable in talking about these issues, the interviewer must appear to be listening. To ensure that full understanding is attained, the interviewer must not only appear to listen, but must actually do so with real concentration.

We let people know we are listening in two important ways non-verbally and verbally.

1 Non-verbal cues

- Eye contact
- Smiling and nodding
- Responding facially
- Attentive posture

2 Verbal

- Encouraging inputs such as 'Yes', 'I see', 'Then?', and so on
- Asking for repetition of any word or name that has been missed
- Checking understanding by paraphrasing what has been said and asking if the interpretation is correct
- Making notes
- Asking questions which show that previous replies have been absorbed

Questioning appropriately may involve using a number of types of question. Some questions will be prepared in advance, but others must be constructed during the interview in response to what has been said. There are a number of different types of question which may be used:

1 *Open questions* – used to leave an open field for the person to answer.

- 'Tell me about . . .'
- 'What kind of work do you like?'
- 'How do you see the future?'

2 *Probing questions* – used to fill in details from generalized replies.

- 'What exactly caused that?'
- 'You referred to an unpleasant incident a few

moments ago, can you tell me exactly what was involved?'

- 'Who was it caused these problems?'

3 *Reflective questions* – used to repeat what has been said or implied to encourage further disclosure. They show an awareness of feelings.

- 'You sound frustrated about that?'
- 'Does dealing with customers often upset you?'
- 'You say he actually made you cry?'

4 *Closed questions* – used to establish specific facts.

- 'Did you ask to be transferred?'
- 'How old were you?'
- 'Which machine was that?'

5 *Comparisons* – used as a preliminary to more probing questions.

- 'Which do you prefer, writing or selling?'
- 'Which did you find easier, WordPerfect or Word?'
- 'Who is the better manager?'

Some questioning approaches are not appropriate, particularly *leading questions*, such as 'You'd like that, wouldn't you?' or 'You'll need training in that, won't you?'

OTHER ASPECTS OF THE INTERVIEW

As well as questioning and listening, there are other aspects of the interview to be considered.

- Ensure that interviews are conducted out of earshot of other people
- Maintain confidentiality
- Make good use of silence, allowing the other person time to think and reply
- Maintain an appropriate distance from the interviewee
- Make lots of notes

You will also need to plan the interview, to some degree,

in advance. It is sometimes worthwhile to prepare a standard list of questions to use with a group of people. Clearly the questions will vary according to the organization and the types of job in question. The following are some possible questions.

- What aspects of your job do you find satisfying?
- What would you change about your job if you could?
- Which aspects of your work interest you least?
- Which aspects of your work do you find most difficult?
- Have you sometimes found it difficult to do your job because of a lack of technical knowledge?
- What training have you had?
- What training do you think would be useful in your present position?
- What training do you wish you had received in the past?
- Have you any skills or knowledge that are not being used in your job?
- How do you know if you are doing a good job?
- What do you think other people think about your performance?
- When do you feel most pressured?

Another possible approach is to concentrate on the anticipated changes in the job. An example of this approach is given in the exercises in the Activities section at the end of this chapter.

Survey Methods

Surveys can be very useful in the gathering of data, including information on attitudes. People usually participate willingly if the completion of a survey form is not too complex or lengthy and if they think some good will come out of the exercise.

When designing a survey you must first make some decisions.

Sample   How many people will you ask? All of them, or just 10 per cent? If not 100 per cent, how can you ensure fair representation? Make sure that you do not end up only asking grade 4 people, or only those in Scotland if you are going to present the results as applying to the whole organization. Political considerations often mean that it is better to survey everyone so that nobody feels left out.

Question format   The main formats available are:

- Freeform: 'What do you think of the training in this company?'
- Multiple choice: 'Which best describes the current position: (a) excellent; (b) satisfactory; (c) unsatisfactory; (d) awful?
- Yes/No: Do you think training has improved over the last two years? (Yes/No)

How   Certain decisions have to be made in terms of how the survey is to be conducted. If you are just trying to get a global picture, then you may choose to make the responses anonymous. More often, you will want to know the job or name of the person concerned so that any identified needs can then be met. If the survey says it is anonymous, but then asks for grade, age and length of service, people will assume that they will be identified from these particulars anyway. Make it clear when and how the form should be returned.

An alternative approach is to 'walk' the survey round. Delivering and collecting by hand will improve the response rate, but at a time cost. You may even want to ask the questions orally and write down the responses, as market researchers often do in shopping centres. Again, this is a slow method best suited for low numbers.

In order to get continued cooperation from people, publish the results and ensure there is no negative comeback on participants.

A sample extract from a survey form is shown in example 1.9.

Appraisal Systems

Many organizations see performance appraisal schemes as an integral part of their employee development strategy. Schemes vary considerably from one organization to another, but almost all of them include the identification of training needs as a key component. Most also consider the longer-term career options available to employees, and allow them to express their preferences. It follows that anyone with responsibility for training and development should influence the design of the scheme and ensure that notice is taken of the information generated by it.

This is not always readily achieved. Sometimes the scheme will focus on short-term performance issues, and line managers may not regard consideration of developmental issues as important. The appraisal may also be considered as confidential within the department concerned. Sometimes the section covering training and development needs is detachable, so that the training function only gets to see the appropriate information. This approach has its merits but excludes the underlying performance issues which contribute towards identifying the training and development needs.

There are many issues to be addressed when designing and implementing an appraisal scheme, and some of the aims of the process may conflict with each other. For example, a scheme linked to the determination of pay increases may inhibit the appraisee from being honest about aspects of the job that he or she finds difficult, whereas it is precisely these aspects that need to be discussed to identify training needs. Care is needed to minimize these conflicts.

Training Needs Survey

This is a survey to determine how well your manager communicates with you. The results will be used to help us determine training needs for managers. All responses will be treated as confidential and no attempt will be made to identify either respondents or their managers.

1. How well does your manager keep you informed of what is going on within your own division?

Very well ☐
Fairly well ☐
Not very well ☐
Not at all ☐

2. How well does your manager keep you informed of what is going on within other divisions?

Very well ☐
Fairly well ☐
Not very well ☐
Not at all ☐

3. How often does your manager organize team meetings?

Daily ☐
More than once a week ☐
Weekly ☐
Twice a month ☐
Monthly ☐
Quarterly ☐
Every six months ☐
Less than every six months ☐
Never ☐

4. How effective are the team meetings?

Very effective ☐
Fairly effective ☐
Not very effective ☐
Completely ineffective ☐

Please add any comments that you feel would be useful.

5. How often does your manager discuss objectives with you before you undertake any training or development activities?

Always ☐
Usually ☐
Sometimes ☐
Rarely ☐
Never ☐
No training ☐

Example 1.9 Extract from a survey

WHO SHOULD BE INVOLVED?

By far the most common arrangement is that employees are appraised by their immediate bosses, but there are many variations on this. In some organizations a second appraisal is conducted by the next higher level in an attempt to ensure any personality conflicts are overcome and to promote improved contact between senior and junior staff. There is a noticeable trend to include inputs into the appraisal process from both peers and subordinates. Each option has implications for both the appraisal process as a whole and also for training need identification in particular. The senior management are looking at performance from their perspective, whereas peers and subordinates may be much more concerned with the softer aspects of performance such as performing as a team member, motivating others or being receptive to other people's ideas.

INCORPORATING THE IDENTIFICATION OF NEEDS INTO APPRAISAL

There are very many different forms in use in very different organizations. Sometimes there is a separate section which looks something like that shown in example 1.10. An alternative approach is to link each assessment of performance and the achievement of objectives to the identification of needs (example 1.11).

Please indicate the most important training and development needs which have been identified.

Learning need   *Method*   *Target date*

Example 1.10 Training and development within appraisal

Performance area	Assessment	Training and/or development implications
1		
2		
3		
etc.		

Next year's objectives	Measure of success	Training and/or development implications
1		
2		
3		
etc.		

Example 1.11 Training and development linked to performance

RAISING EXPECTATIONS

One very real problem with the introduction of appraisal schemes which include the identification of training needs as a core part of their purpose is that expectations are raised. On first introducing a scheme, hundreds of needs may be revealed which were previously hidden. Typically, the training budget cannot cope with all these needs in one go, and so many remain unsatisfied. The result of this is that profound cynicism quickly sets in. Should the same disappointment be repeated in the following year, then the reputation of the scheme as an effective and meaningful process for dealing with needs and aspirations will be permanently damaged. Accordingly, appraisers should be encouraged to:

- prioritize needs
- advise appraisees that some requests may not be met, and why
- actively seek out low-cost or no-cost solutions, such as coaching or reading

There are many other issues to be addressed in the design and implementation of an appraisal scheme. There are a number of good books available which give help to someone who has to manage this task. That by G. C. Anderson (1993) also includes advice on managing the relationship between performance appraisal and career development.

Summary

In this chapter the concept of a 'training need' has been explored with reference to other reasons for wanting to improve performance. The model developed by Boydell (1983) has been outlined – that is, distinguishing between individual, occupational and organizational training needs. The differences between maintenance needs and development needs have also been considered, as has the difference between needs identified proactively and reactively. The ways in which these concepts interact have also been explored.

Methods of identifying needs have been considered under the following headings.

- Job and task analysis
- Skill matrices
- Interviewing
- Survey methods
- Appraisal

All of these methods are resource intensive. Seldom can the trainer operate without the agreement and cooperation of the line management, and often the analysis of training needs must be devolved to the line management.

The trainer must then act as the coordinator of information, as an adviser, and as the instigator of training activity. Time spent identifying training needs is wasted unless those needs are subsequently addressed.

ACTIVITIES

1   Case Study – The factory visit

Mary arrived at the factory in ample time for her interview with Clive Roberts, the personnel manager at Parmell. She had answered the advertisement for a training officer a few weeks before, and was keen to join the Parmell team. She approached the gatehouse and noticed the two security officers chatting in the corner of the room over a copy of a newspaper. She tapped on the window, but the men ignored her. She tapped again, and this time one of them looked up. He sauntered across to the window, still chatting to his colleague as he did so.

'Yes, dear?' he enquired.

After Mary had explained that she had come for an interview, the security officer directed her to reception, and then resumed his chat with his colleague.

'Didn't think we were taking any women on,' she heard him say.

It was a difficult job finding reception, but Mary did so eventually. As she signed in, Mary noticed that the telephone was allowed to ring for a long time before, eventually, a young woman picked it up. 'Hello.' Pause, 'No, this is reception. No. No, I can't transfer you, I don't know how. Bye.'

'Been here before?' asked the receptionist. Mary replied that she had not. 'Well, just be careful as you walk across the yard – some of these forklift drivers go at quite a lick! Anyway, I'll point out the personnel manager's door to you.'

The receptionist propped open the side door with the fire extinguisher and directed Mary across the yard.

As she waited for her interview, Mary overheard the secretary calling someone on the internal telephone.

'Ken? Thank goodness. The photocopier's jammed again. Could you come and have a look? Thanks.' The secretary resumed her keyboard at the computer. Mary noticed that she was copying a typed page of an internal report and commented, 'That looks a lengthy job.'

'Yes. If only they used the same typeface as us, I wouldn't have to do this every month to incorporate the safety report into the personnel report.'

During her interview, Clive Roberts said, 'Well then, Mary, you seem to know a lot about identifying training needs in theory, how about in practice? Have you spotted any here at Parmell?'

What training needs might Mary comment on?

2 Task analysis

Introduction   This activity is most suitable for use with a group of between six and twelve people, but can be adapted for smaller or larger numbers.

Aims   To give practice in the process of task analysis and of the writing of instructions. Precise objectives may be determined by the course tutor.

Method   Divide the class into three teams. Assign each team a task to analyse (example 1.12) with the following brief.

You will be assigned a piece of equipment. Analyse all the steps necessary to take the equipment from the state it is in when given to you to the state required. From this analysis, produce a written set of instructions. This set of instructions will be handed to a member of another group who will read them out to a colleague from the same group who will attempt to follow them precisely.

Timings   Allow 40 minutes to perform the task analysis and prepare the instructions. Allow about five to ten minutes for each activity to be demonstrated, with a similar time for discussion of the learning points which arise.

Variations Allow or forbid the use of diagrams. The activity is more difficult if diagrams are forbidden.

3 Training needs identification by interviewing

Introduction This is a self-generated role-play exercise. It may be conducted in pairs or with observers.

Aims To provide an opportunity for interviewing techniques to be practised.

Method Every participant produces an outline job description and an interviewer's brief. These are then swapped and the interviews are conducted either in pairs or in triads, with participants taking turns to observe, be interviewed or interview.

Timings About 20 minutes to prepare the briefs followed by about ten minutes for people to study the briefs received. The interviews will typical last about ten to 15 minutes. Feedback, discussion and analysis will take a further ten minutes after each interview.

Training needs exercise

Think about the some of people where you work. Select someone who has one major or several minor weaknesses which need to be addressed in order to improve performance. Some of these may be due to training needs, some to poor attitude or motivation. If necessary, exaggerate the problem(s) or combine a few individuals' faults.

1 Prepare a *brief* description of the job.
2 Prepare an interviewer's brief – as if you were looking at the situation from outside and were briefing yourself for the encounter – using the format shown in example 1.13. Use a fictitious name.

Equipment	Initial state	Final state	Safety notes
Flipchart stand	Completely folded down with the pad removed	Fully erected with the pad properly positioned	Involves bending and lifting
Overhead projector and screen	Overhead projector as folded down as possible, facing the wrong way. Screen folded down or out of position	Image correctly projected onto screen	Care with electricity – also avoid the projector being turned on when the mirror is down
Video recorder and monitor	Leads disconnected and monitor/ TV not tuned in. Video cassette in case	Showing a video tape with correctly adjusted volume, etc.	Care with electricity

Example 1.12 Task analysis exercise

3 You will play the character that you have described – someone else will conduct the interview.

Interviewer's brief You are going to talk to someone whose performance is less good than required. His/her manager has left you some notes, but is away from work for some time and cannot be contacted. Try to identify any training needs, but also note any non-training issues.

4 Skill matrix exercise

Introduction   Learners prepare a skill matrix.

Aims   To consolidate learning, and to raise issues for further discussion.

The interviewee's name is: .... (*use a fictitious name*)

He/she has been employed for ....

He/she works as ....

His/her performance is:

....
....
....
....
....
....
....
....
....
....
....

Example 1.13 Interviewer's brief

Method The group selects a suitable area for study and a list of tasks or duties generated. If they are all from the same organization then it may be appropriate to select an actual department. If from different and diverse organizations, then some fairly common activity is selected to use as a simulation. For example, operations concerned with basic car maintenance may be analysed to produce a list ranging from 'fill up with petrol' through 'change wheel' to 'replace clutch'. Participants' names are then listed and they identify themselves as competent or not. If required, they may use a more sophisticated assessment system. Issues related to problems of assessment and the definition of competence will arise and may be discussed. Other possibilities for matrix generation are 'using office equipment', 'looking after babies', and 'preparing a Sunday lunch'. Note that it does not matter if some of the participants have a lot of knowledge whereas others have only a little – the matrix will be more interesting if this is so.

Timings   About 30 minutes for the whole activity.

FURTHER READING

Anderson, A. H. 1993: *Successful training practice: a manager's guide to personnel development.* Oxford: Blackwell Publishers.

Anderson, G. C. 1993: *Managing Performance Appraisal Systems.* Oxford: Blackwell Publishers.

Bartram, S. and Gibson, B. 1994: *Training Needs Analysis. Aldershot: Gower.*

Boydell, T. H. 1983: *A Guide to the Identification of Training Needs.* London: BACIE.

Pearn, M. and Kandola, R. 1988: *Job Analysis: A Practical Guide for Managers.* London: Institute of Personnel Management.

Truelove, S. (ed.) 1995: *The Handbook of Training and Development* (2nd edn). Oxford: Blackwell.

2

Design of Training

Creative minds have always been known to survive any kind of bad training.
                    Anna Freud, Chambers Book of Quotations

Learning Objectives

The purpose of training is expressed through the use of stated aims and objectives. Words such as 'aim', 'objective', 'goal', 'target' and 'purpose' are used in different ways according to the context. There has long been controversy about exactly how objectives should be defined. The current consensus favours the views of those who believe that objectives are meaningless unless they describe terminal behaviours in very precise, measurable and observable terms. I shall start by describing that viewpoint, which is widely held, before considering different attitudes. With regard to training, we can consider the following as usable definitions.

Aim A general statement of the purpose of a programme of training, for example: 'To train journalists to be more effective in the way they manage their time'.

Objective A definition of the behaviour that the person will be able to display at the end of the training, for example: 'The trainee will be able to locate, activate and operate the widget machine so as to produce widgets to the company standard at the rate of 100 units per hour.'
    This approach to writing objectives has been refined

and extensively written about (see, for example, Mager, 1990). Objectives following his rules are sometimes labelled 'Mager-style' objectives and sometimes 'behavioural' objectives. Mager believes that an objective should have three components.

- A definition of the behaviour act
- A definition of the important conditions under which the behaviour is to occur
- A definition of the criterion of acceptable performance

In the United Kingdom the third component of 'criterion' is more usually expressed as 'standards', but the effect is the same.

Obviously, it is easier for precise objectives to be set in terms of speed and accuracy for readily measured outputs (e.g. typing) than for sophisticated behavioural outputs (e.g. motivating people). Nevertheless, statements can be made which give a reasonable indication of what the training is meant to achieve, for example: 'The trainee will be able to initiate conversation with the customer in a friendly and business-like way which will create a positive impression of both the trainee and the company.' With such a statement, whether or not the objective has been met will still be a subjective decision – but at least there is a guideline to judge against.

Note the use of the definite 'will be able to' followed by an active verb. This clearly expresses the required behaviour. Phrasings such as 'should be able to' are considered to be too imprecise. Similarly, words such as 'know', 'understand', or 'appreciate' are considered to be too open to differences in interpretation for use in objectives. Also, they are not observable. How can you tell if someone 'knows' something? Well, you can ask them to state or write what they know. If this is really what is required, then we should say so. Therefore words like 'state' or 'write' should form part of the objective. It can be seen that, if so written, the objective will give us a clear idea of how to approach the measurement necessary to confirm the achievement of the desired learning.

Performance	Conditions	Standards
Mow the lawn	An electric mower in good condition	No areas missed
	Square or rectangular flat lawn	No cuttings left
	Initial grass length 3 cm to 5 cm	Clear, straight-line pattern
	Dry grass	No scalping
		At the rate of 600 sq m per hour

Example 2.1 Components of an objective

Performance	Test of performance
To type a business letter	In an office situation using Word for Windows from a handwritten original of 400 words at 40 words per minute or faster with no more than ten errors before spell checking, and no more than two errors after spell checking

Example 2.2 Test of performance

If a lot of detail is required for a training programme to be constructed, objectives must be stated for each component part of the programme. These are sometimes termed 'learning unit objectives' and can be expressed with whatever precision is required in terms of standards and also with reference to the conditions under which the performance is required. They may be written in three-column format as shown in example 2.1. An alternative is to combine the conditions and standards into a test of performance that will indicate whether the desired performance outcome has been achieved (example 2.2).

• Make sure the objective states what the trainee will be

doing when demonstrating his or her achievement, and how you will know when he or she is doing it
- Define the important conditions
- Define the standards of performance required
- Write as many separate objectives as are needed to achieve clarity
- Let the learner know the objectives

DIFFERENT VIEWS

Some jobs are very complex, and the time spent writing Mager-style objectives can be enormous. Educational research reported by Davies (1976) suggests that specific behavioural objectives are no more effective than general objectives. Other writers believe you should include the learning process as part of a well-written objective. The following quotations are taken from Knowles (1990) who explores the topic more fully than it is possible to do here.

> Objectives should also be so formulated that there are clear distinctions among learning experiences required to attain different behaviours. (Taba, 1962)

> Objectives are developmental, representing roads to travel rather than terminal points. (Taba, 1962)

> I do not intend or expect one outcome or one cluster of outcomes but *any one* of several, a plurality. (Schwab, 1971)

These views emphasize both the unpredictability of learning and the importance of considering the processes which lead to learning outcomes. The ultimate limitation of Mager-style objectives is that they may lead us to take a trainer-centred approach. We control what will be learned as precisely as possible. I believe that this approach is wholly valid when considering the training of tasks such as operating a photocopier or using a lathe. However, more complex and 'softer' skills such as counselling or leading a group discussion benefit little from such attention to detail, and may even be harmed by it. If the trainer is taking a facilitative approach and drawing on the skills and knowledge present in the group, and responding to the issues that arise from the group, then the precise learning outcomes must be different on every occasion, if only to a small extent. To reject learning simply because it does not fit in with a pre-ordained prediction seems rather limiting.

A balance must be struck. It is possible to become very vague about what will be learned, or to use phrases such as 'a voyage of self-discovery'. Busy line managers tend to be impatient with that approach. Not unreasonably, they want to know what the objectives of the programme are before committing their time or that of other people. Accordingly, the declared objectives of a training event often represent the minimum learning that will take place and can act as a reminder to the trainer that this has been promised. Whatever promises you make in the declared objectives, you must try to ensure that these promises are kept.

Adult Learning

The process of learning is a highly complex one and many theories have been put forward to help us understand it. Knowles (1990) lists some 61 propounders and a further 33 interpreters of learning theory. For the training practitioner, an understanding of one or two theories or models of learning can be very useful.

Although there is no single, unequivocally accepted, definition of precisely what the word 'learning' means, most authorities agree that learning is about 'changing behaviour'. We will first consider a well-established model of learning that can be very useful in some situations.

CONDITIONING THEORY

Although developed from observations of animal learning, the process which is termed conditioning has been demonstrated to apply to human learning in very many instances. Its most eminent advocate as a theory was Skinner (1968) who conducted research into the process over many years. The principle by which conditioning works is that behaviour which is rewarded (or reinforced) is more likely to recur. Behaviour which is punished (or negatively reinforced) will tend to occur less. The desired behaviour is conditioned to occur as a result of a particular stimulus.

This is the principle used to train a dog to bark in response to a particular blast on a whistle. At the beginning, much patience is needed as the dog does not understand what it is supposed to do. If the trainer blows the whistle and the dog barks, it receives a reward, such as a biscuit. No bark, no reward. No whistle, no reward for barking. Eventually, the connection is established. The reward may now be given only intermittently, but the behaviour will tend to persist. Also, the reward may change to a pat on the head or verbal praise. The behaviour will persist – assuming the dog regards the new reward as a positive experience.

Human beings can learn in the same way. Small children are rewarded with praise for the desired behaviour, and punished by being told off, or possibly smacked, for 'bad' behaviour. Immediately a problem arises when dealing with adult learners. Being praised inappropriately is not rewarding; it is irritating. Being told off is often not acceptable, and being smacked certainly isn't! Therefore, great care must be taken in this process. The frequency and style of praise must be geared to the individual learner. Often the reward can be self-administered. Providing that the learners are given the information to know whether or not they have done something well, then they can give themselves a notional 'well done'. The reward process can also be built into a learning task. Study any good computer game aimed at children. Success at learning the game is periodically rewarded by points, secret levels, progress, fanfares, passwords or whatever other device the creators have dreamed up. The motivational effect of these on some players is very powerful. The fact that others seem not to respond demonstrates that the reward must be a reward *to that individual learner.*

The other limitation of a conditioning approach is that it is best suited to the teaching of simple operations or sequences of operations. It is not an adequate approach when dealing with situations that require an understanding of complex concepts, underlying principles, or problem solving (other than to predetermined formulae). Before considering other models of learning, it is worth considering a simple but valuable way of looking at the ways people learn.

THREE WAYS OF LEARNING

A system developed by Sylvia Downs in the 1980s is to place learning into one of three categories (see Truelove, 1995; Downs, 1995). This is the memorizing–understanding–doing (MUD) taxonomy. The basic concept is that all learning tasks are comprised of one, two or all three of these components. Identifying the ways in which things are learned is an important first step in the design of training programmes, activities and materials. The MUD system distinguishes three different groups of things to be learned, each of which uses different methods.

- *Facts* which need to be *memorized*
- *Concepts* which need to be *understood*
- *Physical skills* which need to be experienced by *doing*

If the nature of the learning is misunderstood, then the training method applied will be inappropriate.

- You can get someone to repeat a phrase from a textbook until it is word perfect; but there may be no understanding

- You can explain in detail to someone the process of juggling, perhaps using slow-motion video, until they understand what is happening; but it does not mean that that person will be able to juggle
- You can teach someone how to operate a microwave oven; but he or she may not be able to name the component parts of the oven

There are various ways to help people cope with all three types of learning.

MEMORIZING

The main mechanism for straightforward memorization is through repetition. It is the trainer's task to organize repetition so that it is not boring. Exercises can be devised which repeat information in new ways and require the learner to use the new information. However, it can be very helpful to think of memory aids which assist this process, such as the following.

Link or group items 'This is another way of affecting the appearance. So, as with "character", "paragraph" is found under Format.'

Break into parts Make sure no one item is too big for comfortable memorization. Teach part one, then part two, and then combine them before moving to part three.

Mnemonics Special aids such as acronyms or rhymes can be incredibly helpful in some instances. For example, the way in which most British people remember how many days there are in each month – 'Thirty days hath September . . .' – or the order of the spectrum – 'Richard of York Gained Battle in Vain' (Red, Orange, Yellow, Green, Blue, Indigo, Violet). If you can think of a nice, easy-to-learn mnemonic, then you can help people to memorize lists or sequences much better.

People memorize best when they concentrate. Concentration is crucial to the memorization process.

Concentration can be impaired by tiredness and improved by a feeling of commitment to the learning task. People must also be allowed time to reflect on what they have learned. Therefore, resist lengthy training sessions, particularly after the trainee has been hard at work for some hours.

UNDERSTANDING

Helping people to understand something is not always easy. We cannot understand for them. What we can do is to explain carefully, and to encourage analysis by asking questions. Downs (1995) gives us four keys to understanding.

1 Purposes – why something is as it is; what it is trying to do
2 Comparisons – comparing and contrasting with other experiences; identifying similarities and differences
3 Viewpoints – imagining things from other directions, or from others' viewpoints
4 Problems – what could go wrong and how would we overcome that?

We can also aid understanding by ensuring that the use of unfamiliar jargon is minimized and by relating the learning to what the trainee already knows and understands. Understanding is the most difficult form of learning to assess. Whereas memory can be checked by asking for facts to be repeated, and doing can be checked by observation, understanding requires a variety of checking processes. The keys to understanding given above can also serve as the keys to checking understanding. One approach that does not work is to ask. 'Do you understand?'

LEARNING TO DO SOMETHING

Learning to do something is easier if you are clear as to the purpose of what you are trying to achieve, know relevant procedures or rules and are allowed adequate practice of the skills involved.

Because unlearning can be difficult, it is important to get the movements right from the start. Often professional sports coaches prefer to teach people who are absolutely new to the sport rather than people who have picked up bad habits already.

Learners often get to a stage where they do not seem to improve much. This is termed a 'learning plateau'. Trainers may need to support and encourage learners through this stage. When someone begins to learn a piece of skilled behaviour, he or she has to concentrate on memorizing a series of movements, perhaps linking these to sensory cues. Eventually, these conscious actions become automatic and this is how people get off the plateau. This is often the stage when people are unconsciously learning to use information from muscles as well as from eyes and ears. Using this muscle information is much quicker than using other cues.

Experiential Learning

It is common for training courses to be described as 'practical' (perhaps workshop based) or 'theoretical' (probably classroom based). However, we know that the good workshop instructor will relate the practical to the theoretical, and the good academic teacher will illustrate theoretical points by reference to practical examples. Similarly, we have probably all experienced training which we thought was very good but which we quickly forgot or found when we came to use the learning that it did not seem to apply to our situation. Among many theorists who have studied human learning, the work of Kolb (1974, 1984); has been widely adopted as the most useful way of helping trainers to design learning events. Kolb developed a four stage cycle to describe the ideal sequence for effective learning to take place (example 2.3).

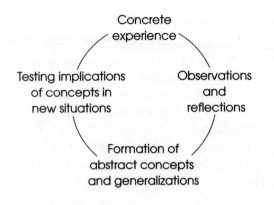

Concrete experience

Testing implications of concepts in new situations

Observations and reflections

Formation of abstract concepts and generalizations

Source: Kolb (1974) p. 28. Reproduced by permission of David A. Kolb

Example 2.3 The Kolb learning cycle

The four stages should always follow the same sequence but may start at any one of the stages.

Concrete experience   This is were the learner is personally involved in something and gains feedback as to how well or how badly he or she has performed a task. For this to be useful as a learning experience the learner must be aware of what is happening. The trainer may help by pointing out various cues, for example, 'The steering may feel less responsive now'.

Reflective observation   It is not enough simply to have an experience in order to learn. Without reflecting on the experience it may quickly be forgotten or its learning potential lost. It is from the feelings and thoughts emerging from this reflection and analysis that generalizations or concepts may be generated. If this does not happen, the learner may become skilled at the specific task being taught but cannot generalize from one situation to other situations. This is the stage of the cycle that may benefit from a trainer asking questions to stimulate thought and from discussion.

Abstract conceptualization It is only from generalizations and conceptual understanding that new situations can be tackled effectively. This stage involves learners developing a deeper understanding of what they have learned. It is often helped by input from an instructor about a theory or a model which can be applied in a variety of situations. If the learner does not understand the connection between the theory and the practice, then he or she will be unable to make use of the theory in the work situation.

Active experimentation For learning to result in changed behaviour it is not sufficient to learn new concepts and develop new generalizations. The implications of the newly learned concepts must be tested out in new situations. The learner must make the link between theory and action by planning for that action and carrying it out.

Example

1 A trainee nurse might start learning to lift a patient by trying to lift a dummy out of a wheelchair (*active experimentation*)
2 She finds this difficult and fails (*concrete experience*)
3 The instructor encourages reflection by questioning: 'How did that feel? Was it hurting your back?' (*reflective observation*)
4 The nurse then reads a manual about lifting techniques (*abstract conceptualization*)
5 The nurse now tries out one of the techniques on the dummy (*active experimentation*)
6 The nurse notices how much more effective the new method is (*concrete experience*)
7 She discusses her experiences with some other trainees (*reflective observation*)
8 The instructor now asks the group to look in the manual and to identify all possible methods suitable

for lifting an unconscious patient (*abstract conceptualization*)

and so on.

The important point about experiential learning theory is that experience alone is not enough. We must think about what we have done, and what we are going to do, to maximize learning. We must also understand the underlying principles concerning whatever we are learning if we are to be able to work out appropriate courses of action for ourselves.

The other implication from Kolb's concept is that learning actually requires more than one skill from the learner. The four stages of the learning cycle require us to operate in a different learning mode. Kolb found that people differ in their comparative ability to operate in each of the four modes. He developed a questionnaire, the Learning Styles Inventory, which allows individuals to look at their own preferences and profiles (see Kolb, Rubin and Osland (1995)).

In the United Kingdom, the concept of learning styles is more usually associated with the work of Honey and Mumford (1986). Honey and Mumford took Kolb's learning cycle and developed a questionnaire which produces scores for four learning styles. This is a different set of styles to that produced by Kolb, and the interested reader should refer to Honey and Mumford (1986) for an explanation of their reasoning for adopting this different approach as well as a thorough description of how the concept of learning styles may be used. I will not attempt to give an explanation here, but many trainers find the concept extremely useful for tailoring course designs to suit particular groups of learners. Once the manual has been purchased, the Learning Styles Questionnaire may be reproduced 'as often as you wish', which is very helpful.

USING THE CYCLE

Of course, theoretical ideas, like those of Kolb, can very easily be seen as irrelevant to practical training. The learning cycle is a useful starting point in the design process. If it is borne in mind, then worthwhile learning experiences are more likely to be produced. In general, the trainer will often find that his or her greatest contribution is in ensuring that sufficient reflection takes place for the fundamental aspects of the learning to be internalized. DeGeus (in Kolb et al., 1995) states that: 'Research on learning styles has shown that managers on the whole are distinguished by very strong active experimentation skills and are very weak on reflective observation skills.'

The challenge for the trainer is to make such managers reflect without alienating them. If they see the trainer as an ivory tower thinker, then they may react negatively to the whole process of reflection. They will become impatient to get on with the next activity. As in many things, a balance must be struck.

Designing Learning Events

WHAT IS DESIGN?

Earl (1987) defines design as:

> The plan, structure and strategy of instruction used, conceived so as to produce learning experiences that lead to pre-specified learning goals.

In turn, the term 'learning experience' may need to be considered. Earl gives a definition by Tyler (1949):

> A learning experience refers to the interaction between the learner and the external conditions in the environment to which he can react. Learning takes place through the active behaviour of the student; it is what he does that he learns not what the teacher does.

This is an important point. Although giving people information through presentations and handouts has its value, it is getting people to do things that is really effective.

FIRST STAGES OF DESIGN

Assess learning needs and from these determine objectives, at the same time considering practicalities concerned with time and resources available. Although many texts will encourage you to define the objectives precisely at this stage, most trainers leave the detailed writing of objectives until later. The questions which follow will all influence what will be achievable.

- Who will the learners be? What are the individual differences? What are their expectations? What style of training will they respond best to? What are they used to?
- What is the nature of the learning? Is it a matter of memory, understanding or doing? What activities or resources are needed?
  - (a) *Memory* Lists, handouts, presentations, activities that require memorization, etc.
  - (b) *Understanding* Lessons, discussions, case studies, role playing, exercises, etc.
  - (c) *Doing* Demonstration, skill practice, role playing, dismantling and reassembly, etc.

We are now in a position to consider what resources exist to meet these needs and what must be created or modified. It is very often possible to find good commercial activities which can be used as they stand. On other occasions you can take the idea and modify it to suit your particular purpose. A decent library of books and commercially produced exercises and case studies can be invaluable as a starting point. Sometimes, though, it is better to start from scratch and think up your own ideas and write your own material. The old saying that 'necessity is the mother of invention' applies as much to the origin of good training ideas as it does to anything else. Do not underestimate your own ability to be creative.

When a good solution has been identified, subject it to the 'three Es test'. Ask yourself if the activity will be:

- effective – will it work?
- enjoyable – will it get a positive response, or be seen as tedious?
- efficient – Even if effective and enjoyable, is it worth the time taken? Or could a shorter activity achieve the same results?

Ideally, try out or 'pilot' the activity in a non-critical situation, perhaps with colleagues, before using it with 'real' learners. Also, be prepared to revise and refine the activity in the light of experience, suggestions from participants, and as a result of the formal evaluation system.

This process is summarized in example 2.4.

Scheduling Begin with the fixed elements – meals, normal working hours, etc. These considerations are especially important if there is little chance of changing them.

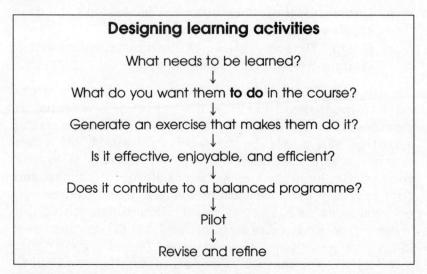

Example 2.4 Designing learning activities

Consider what needs to be learned first. Start with small units and build up to more complex activities. Later elements should consolidate earlier learning in a cohesive way.

Mornings are generally better for theory; afternoons for activity.

Balance   The aims and objectives should be used to determine how much time ought to be devoted to each topic. In part, the time spent will be perceived as an indication of the topic's importance. Thus a two-day selection interviewing course which devoted only 15 minutes to the topic of sex discrimination might give the impression that sex discrimination was not considered to be an important topic, even if it were possible to put across the key points adequately within that time.

There should also be a mixture and balance of training methods. Too much input is tedious. Too much action with little time for discussion or reflection is not good for learning. Too many self-analysis questionnaires, videos, case studies, role plays or games can all give a feeling of monotony to the programme. Chapter 3 discusses many of the methods available to trainers.

Facilitating group formation   Unless a course consists of an existing, fully coherent group, a process of group formation will occur. The longer the course, the more important this is. Even on short courses the group will develop. Its capacity to tackle exercises increases, as does its confidence to challenge and question. Early activities should be relatively short, not too difficult, and not promote animosity between group members. Activities should help people to identify with each other rather than cause conflict or embarrassment.

Timings   Although this has already been considered, the design will have to be modified as the material is developed. If time is short, long exercises – even if effective – will have to be discarded in favour of shorter ways of achieving the learning. If you are struggling to fill the time available, then the best solution is to shorten the course. There is a tendency to think that a course must be either (say) three days or four days. Could it be three days and three hours? Is a three-hour session likely to be unacceptable? If so, could each day be extended by an hour to fit in the learning? What would the reaction to that be?

A good test is to refer back to the objectives. Decide which of them are essential, which less so, and which could be left out altogether. A common way of doing this is to prioritize the objectives.

- **Must know**
- **Should know**
- **Nice to know**

Training is often a compromise between three factors. The *range* of learning which will be covered, the *depth* to which the coverage will go, and the *time* which will be taken. This may be considered as a balance (example 2.5). If more range is required, then either the time must be increased or the depth reduced. Similarly, if more depth

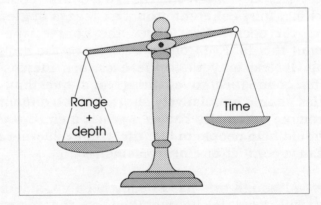

Example 2.5 Balancing the range and depth of learning with available time

is required then either the range of coverage must be decreased or the time must increase.

Finally After the design has been produced, modified and refined, leave it for a few days. Go back to it and think it all through again. Very often good ideas take time to filter through, or ideas that seemed great at the moment of inspiration look rather lame a few days later.

Once the course has been run, revise it and amend it further. Of course utilize the feedback from participants, but your own feelings and perceptions will also be important in assessing what needs to be changed. Many experienced trainers find that it usually takes about three courses before they are happy with a design.

More guidance on how to tackle the writing of material is given in chapter 3.

Lesson Plans

The purpose of a lesson plan is to guide the trainer through the training event. A lesson plan is an outline of what you intend to happen, in the required sequence, and a reminder of what is required to make it happen. It is particularly important when more than one trainer is delivering the same session or course. If things are not written down, then it is likely that people will end up receiving different messages or that version A of one course overlaps with version B of another. Even if you are the only person to be delivering the training, it is still good practice to write down what you intend to do. Consider also that, in months or years to come, you might want to hand over the course to someone else. This is so much easier if a good lesson plan is available.

The first part of the lesson plan is primarily administrative. A sample is given in example 2.6.

After the administrative details are completed some sort of lesson outline, training brief, or tutor guide is required. This is prepared to the degree of detail required.

Lesson Plan

Course title:...

Lesson title:...

Code: ....

Prepared by:...

Date:...

Learning objectives:

Target audience:

Maximum class size: Minimum class size:

Essential prior knowledge:

Learner preparation:

Learner materials:

Handout list:

Equipment:

Duration:

Evaluation/validation:

Comments:

Example 2.6 Lesson plan

It should not be a script, but a reminder of what to do and when. A sample format is given in example 2.7.

Although a detailed guide like this is highly important when preparing for delivery, many trainers find it easier to work with their own handwritten notes as simple prompts. These can be highlighted with colour, or appropriate symbols can be used. A rough working plan may look like example 2.8. This example shows how a full day could be noted on page of A4, which is how I prefer to work. Other people use cards, or work from the full guide. There is no right way; develop whatever way suits you or your team.

Structuring Programmes

We have looked at some of the ways in which training needs can be identified, and we have looked at the way in which the design of learning events is approached. I am using the term 'programme' to design a series of learning events. These may follow on from each other one after the other, or they may be separated in time. The key thing about a programme is that it is designed as a coherent whole. The process of preparing a programme to address needs at the occupational level may be thought of as comprising ten stages.

Stage 1 Enlist support and gain commitment from the key people. This may be the jobholders, but will always involve the line management. Do not embark on a lengthy analytical and design process before enlisting such support.

Stage 2 Examine and describe the job as previously explained in chapter 1 or using whatever other method you prefer.

Stage 3 Prepare a knowledge and skill breakdown, again as explained in chapter 1. If you prefer, you may use MUD

Team management

Time	Session	Objectives	Method	Materials
9.00	Welcome and introduction	Gain commitment to the course Create appropriate climate	Paired interviewing (15 mins) Report back (c. 20 mins) Tutor gives own details (5 mins) Domestics (5 mins) -fire/toilets/first aid/smoking/timings/lunch (5 mins) Course outline (5 mins)	OHP of fire procedure TM1 programme
9.55	Clarifying objectives	To enable learners to influence the course content with regard to their own perceived needs	Split into two or three groups (c. 5 in each) Groups to discuss course outline. To identify any points apparently not covered plus any aspects of particular interest to them plus any aspects not interested in. Groups to make notes on flipchart and feed back to plenary. 20 mins syndicate 20 mins plenary	Flipchart, paper, pens
10.35	Coffee			
10.50	What is a leader?	To identify the skills and characteristics of successful leadership	Split group into threes/fours Ask: Think of four successful leaders from politics, sport, warfare, work List qualities on flipchart Report back in 15 minutes	Flipchart, paper, pens

Example 2.7 Tutor guide

9.00	Intro.
→Do	Paired interviewing
9.25	Input on new policy (OHP 1–4)
9.45	
→Do	Syndicates to discuss
9.55	Plenary
	Chart and discuss
10.10	
Video	'Tomorrow today'
10.40	Discuss
10.50	Coffee
etc.	

Example 2.8 Working plan

analysis or any other system which fits with the kind of work you are dealing with. Sometimes an extra category of 'attitude' is added to the knowledge/skill breakdown.

Stage 4 Produce a syllabus. A training syllabus is simply a composite list of the learning identified as necessary at stage 3. It may be helpful to divide the list up under the headings chosen (e.g., memory; understanding; doing). It may also be found that certain areas of learning are present in a number of different tasks. These may be considered as basic to the job, and it may be useful to separate these out at this stage so that they can be given special attention.

Stage 5 All the learning identified in the syllabus must now be defined more closely. Objectives should be written with as clearly defined standards and conditions as necessary for this stage. Alternatively, use competence criteria if that is the language your organization prefers.

Stage 6 It is also useful to prepare a statement of pre-entry requirements for the training programme. This has two components.

• What skills, knowledge or experience must someone

have before they can start the current training? (e.g., must they have held a full driving licence for at least six months?)

- What personal qualities or abilities must they possess before they can start the current training? (e.g., must they have normal colour vision?)

The purpose of doing this is so that you can be fairly clear in your own mind about what you can assume learners will already know and what their minimum existing capabilities will be.

Ensure that no requirements have the effect of causing either direct or indirect discrimination (e.g., 'must have been a boy scout').

Stage 7   The various objectives or syllabus components can now be played around with. A rough idea of the methods to be used and the duration of the learning activity can be assigned. As more thought is given to this process, it may become apparent that one activity will serve more than one learning objective or that more than one activity will be required to achieve the level of learning required.

Thought must also be given to sequencing the learning. Some things must be learned before others can be. There will also be considerations to do with practicalities.

- Room availability
- Equipment availability
- Optimum group size
- Taking people away from their existing work
- How large a group of newly trained people can the operational areas absorb?

You may also want to consider various formats for the programme. If the programme looks like it should last for six days, it may be more sensible to break it into two three-day, three two-day, or six one-day sessions. There are always advantages and disadvantages with whatever format is chosen, so think all the options through and discuss them with the people who matter – line managers and/or the learners.

At some point the learning events which have been designed to produce the desired outcomes must be designed in detail. The process is still interactive at this point in that the precise content of one session will affect and be affected by the content of other sessions. Constant rethinking will occur as the design is worked on until a sound programme is reached. The objectives may need to be revised to more closely reflect what you now think will be possible. This may be viewed as being the wrong way round, but it is in fact what most trainers actually do.

It is often useful to produce an outline programme for issuing to learners or their managers. This does not need all the detail found in the tutor guide, and is not so precisely timed. The sample training programme shown in example 2.9 also has a code referring to the appropriate lesson plan and tutor guide.

Stage 8 Discuss the design with the those people whose support you sought at stage 1. Be prepared to amend your

Week 1	Session title	Code	By
Day 1	Data lists	K1	AS
	Sales leads and market coverage	K2	AS
	Demonstrations	S1	G
			H
Day 2	List management	K3	AS
	Pricing policies	K3	AS
	Marketing materials	K4	G
			H
Day 3	Job costing system	K5	JP
	Credit verification	K6	AS
	Telephone skills 1	S2	G
			H
	etc.		

Example 2.9 Sample training programme

design to keep their support, but try to defend the points which you think are important.

Stage 9 Produce the materials.

Stage 10 Agree and publish dates a reasonable time in advance. Book the room(s), venue, catering, equipment and videos in good time and in writing. Good luck!

Summary

This chapter has attempted to set out the processes involved with the design of training events. First, the writing of objectives was considered with reference to the work of Mager (1990). The preparation of precise behavioural objectives is considered to be very important by many people involved in training, although others see limitations in this approach. Being able to write precise objectives is a fundamental requirement of the modern trainer, even if he or she sometimes prefers not to do so.

Learning processes have also been considered. Conditioning theory has been outlined, as was the MUD taxonomy developed by Downs (1995). Experiential learning theory, as developed by Kolb (1974, 1984) and Kolb et al. (1995) was also described. Of course, these theories and models are of no consequence if they are not used. Practical advice has been given as to how to design learning events, plan lessons and structure programmes. The models and theories given should allow a better understanding of how to approach these activities in order to produce effective learning.

ACTIVITIES

1 Training objectives

The following are attempts to write the performance elements of training objectives. Indicate which ones describe an observable and measurable behaviour.

	Yes	No
1 Name six motor insurance companies operating in the UK	☐	☐
2 Know the principles of fire prevention	☐	☐
3 Be aware of how viruses are introduced into computers	☐	☐
4 List the ten biggest-selling cars	☐	☐
5 Understand the way a laser printer operates	☐	☐
6 Load and fire a pistol	☐	☐
7 Speak clearly on the telephone	☐	☐
8 Appreciate the factors affecting trainee motivation	☐	☐
9 Recall the names of the main board	☐	☐
10 Apply paint as required	☐	☐
11 State how to trigger the alarm	☐	☐
12 Restore antique furniture	☐	☐

2 Learning cycle exercise

Think about a training course which you are involved in as a trainer. If you do not currently run any training courses, think about a programme you have attended as a learner. Analyse the programme, or a section of the programme, in terms of Kolb's learning cycle. If any parts of the cycle are missing, what could be done to correct this?

3 MUD analysis exercise

Introduction A simple exercise designed to show how MUD can be used in practice.

Aims To allow learners to appreciate the way in which MUD can be used in the early stages of programme design.

Method Divide the group into teams of three or four people. Ask them to select a job for analysis of which they all have some knowledge. For example, the job of a bar-tender, or waiter/waitress. They should first of all generate a list of activities within the job. These must then be categorized as requiring learning primarily by memory, or understanding, or doing. Answers are then compared and discussed in a plenary session.

Timings Twenty minutes in small groups. About twenty minutes discussion and analysis in a plenary session.

4 Programme design exercise

Introduction This is a substantial exercise which consolidates many of the learning points covered in sections 1 and 2.

Aims To allow learners to apply the techniques in a real job programme design exercise.

Method This activity works best in groups of four to six people. All instructions are given below.

Timings Depending on the complexity of the job, the degree of detail required and how the programme is presented, between two and five hours.

From within your group, select a volunteer from an organization which recruits into a particular job category on a regular basis. This should be a job which typically takes between two and six weeks for new starters to learn to a reasonable level of proficiency. It is better if no formal training programme currently exists. The volunteer must be familiar with the operations within the job.

• As a group, use interviewing techniques to analyse the skill and knowledge that must be learned within this initial period to attain proficiency

- Prepare a syllabus
- Write objective statements for three of these syllabus items
- Decide on appropriate training methods and prepare an outline training programme which includes timings and methods for the whole syllabus
- Present your programme – being prepared to justify the decisions taken with regard to the content, timings and methods used

FURTHER READING

Davies, I. K. 1976: *Objectives in Curriculum Design*. Maidenhead: McGraw-Hill.

Downs, S. 1995: *Learning at Work*. London: Kogan Page.

Earl, T. 1987: *The Art and Craft of Course Design*. London: Kogan Page.

Honey, P. and Mumford, A. 1986: *The Manual of Learning Styles*. Maidenhead: Peter Honey.

Knowles, M. 1990: *The Adult Learner – A Neglected Species* 4th ed. Houston: Gulf.

Kolb, D. A. 1974: *On Management and the Learning Process*. In Kolb, D. A. Rubin, I. M. and McIntyre, J. M., *Organizational Psychology: A book of readings* (2nd edn). Englewood Cliffs: Prentice-Hall.

Kolb, D. A. 1984: *Experiential Learning: Experience as the Source of Learning and Development*. Englewood Cliffs: Prentice-Hall.

Kolb, D. A., Rubin, I. M. and Osland, J. S. 1995: *Organizational Behaviour: An Experiential Approach* (6th edn). Englewood Cliffs: Prentice-Hall.

Mager, R. F. 1990: *Measuring Instructional Results* (2nd edn). London: Kogan Page.

Rae, L. 1995: *Techniques of Training* (3rd edn). Aldershot: Gower.

Skinner, B. F. 1968: *The Technology of Teaching*. New York: Appleton-Century-Crofts.

Truelove, S. (Ed.) 1995: *The Handbook of Training and Development* (2nd edn). Oxford: Blackwell.

3

▰

Preparing Material

The secret of teaching is to appear to have known all your life what you learned this afternoon.

Anon., Chambers Book of Quotations

Visual Aids

Although the presentation of information is not always the most important task of a trainer, it is often a key part of a training event, and it is certainly a part by which the overall quality of the trainer may be judged. The delivery of information is dealt with in chapter 4. In this section we will consider what is involved in the preparation of visual aids.

WHY BOTHER?

- Visual aids make it easier for people to retain information. In most (but not all) classroom learning the two main senses that will be used are hearing and vision. To fail to make use of the sense of vision as a way of getting information across is unnecessarily limiting.
- Visual aids are often time-savers when you are putting across certain concepts. A diagrammatic representation of a process is often much more readily understood than a verbal explanation.
- They add emphasis, variety and humour to a learning session.
- They help the trainer to remember what to say. You

can use prepared visual aids to guide yourself through a session.

- They take people's eyes off you. If you feel nervous at the start of a training session, put up a visual aid and stand back. They will not be looking at you now, and this will help you to relax.

Whilst the range of possible aids is quite extensive, and new technologies are continuing to evolve, I will concentrate on the three most widely available formats for the delivery of visual information.

- The flipchart
- The whiteboard
- The overhead projector

These items are found in nearly every training room, and the flipchart and overhead projector are readily available in most hotels or other venues used for training. First, we will consider the advantages and disadvantages associated with each of these aids.

FLIPCHARTS

Advantages

- They can be used anywhere. There is no need for a power point or special lighting conditions. Apart from the ones which hang from rails, they all are reasonably portable. They can be moved around the room, taken on to the lawn or turned away from the group.
- They are easy and straightforward to use.
- They often have a whiteboard surface (useful if the paper runs out).
- They are cheap to buy, usually last for years and have little to go wrong.
- The information written on them can be retained for future use or reference.
- They are good for 'live' use. Pages can be turned quickly backwards or forwards; they can be torn off and stuck on the walls or on special rail systems.

Disadvantages

- Unless it is done very carefully, flipcharts prepared in advance can look rather scruffy and amateurish.
- Prepared flipcharts are bulky to carry and are easily damaged in transit. Once rolled up they are hard to get flat again.
- The stands are quite heavy and difficult to carry – even the portable ones.
- They consume a lot of paper. Although the paper is not very expensive, this is still a cost (as are the marker pens), and an ample supply must always be kept in stock. Some people are upset at heavy paper usage for environmental reasons.

WHITEBOARDS

Advantages

- They are usually much bigger than flipcharts, which can often be a major advantage.
- Ordinary ones are not expensive to buy, and have very low running costs.
- Some expensive whiteboards have a built-in photo-copying facility and wind on mechanism.
- Some have a flipchart section built on.

Disadvantages

- You have to stop and clean them when they are full. You often get your hands dirty doing this.
- If you use the wrong (permanent) marker pens on them you are in trouble.
- Writing neatly on a large whiteboard is not easy.
- Most whiteboards are fixed to the wall and, although some are mounted on framework with castors, they are usually quite heavy.

OVERHEAD PROJECTORS

Advantages

- The slides are very portable if travelling between sites. They are also easy to store.
- The projectors are fairly portable within a building, and some are truly portable in that they fold down and are equipped with a carrying handle.
- They give a large and easily seen image.
- Slides can be prepared in advance. Modern software and colour printers mean that professional-looking results are obtainable by most people at a realistic cost.
- They can be really good for presenting graphical data and pictorial information.
- You can choose to sit down or stand when using an overhead projector.

Disadvantages

- You may be restricted by the need to be near a power point. Trailing flexes are a safety hazard.
- They take up a lot of room as there must be room for the image to be projected. The screen may be fixed, reducing your room layout options. If the screen is portable the presence of doors and windows may mean limited choice of position.
- They are quite expensive to buy and consume expensive bulbs. Spares must always be kept at hand.
- They get very dirty, and few people can be bothered to clean them. Some in use (particularly at hotels) are extremely old and battered, which can lead to problems with the projected image.

PREPARING VISUAL AIDS

Flipcharts Flipcharts are at their best when used for live recording of contributions from the group, or for writing up information as you go along. However, there are some occasions when advance preparation is appropriate. Although the following tips may be helpful, there is no need to regard such ideas as golden rules, never to be broken.

- Use every second page only. This will prevent what you have written on a previous page showing through.
- Take the paper off the stand and lay it down flat on a table before you start. Use a T-square to get straight lines.
- Block capitals are usually easier to write neatly, and easier to read, than lower-case letters.
- Use colour for emphasis and variety but don't overdo it as it can be visually messy and confusing. Avoid light colours, as they are harder to read.
- Drawings can look very effective on flipcharts. If you are a poor artist but have a picture you want to put on a flipchart, then you can cheat.
  - Trace the image on to an acetate
  - Project the image on to the flipchart using an overhead projector
  - Trace round the image with a marker pen
- Make bookmarks on the flipchart pad by marking pages with folded corners, paperclips or Post-it notes.

Perhaps have a second flipchart or a whiteboard to use as a scribbling pad so that you don't lose your place on your prepared pad.

Whiteboards Unless the whiteboard can be turned around, any advance work will be immediately visible to the group. However, if this does not matter, then it can be sensible to prepare in advance. Many of the points listed above for the flipchart apply to the whiteboard and there are some additional points.

- Always clean the whiteboard as thoroughly as possible before you start.
- Take care to write in straight lines. Some whiteboards have faint lines or grids which are very helpful. Other-

wise, try projecting a ruler on to the board with an overhead projector. As you finish a line of text, tilt the head of the projector down until the ruler is at the next line down, and so on.

- Use dry marker pens, not permanent pens.
- You can stick pictures on to whiteboards with tape or Blu-tack. Some whiteboards are metal, and then magnets can be used.

Overhead projectors Slides used on the overhead projector are variously referred to as transparencies, acetates, viewfoils, or slides. They may be prepared freehand using special pens, by photocopying on to special acetate sheets or by printing directly on to acetates compatible with your computer's printer. There are a number of other technologies in use. Increasingly common is the projection of images directly from a computer via various special devices. The general rules apply whatever method is used.

- Transparencies should be concise. Do not project a full text, but rather key points which remind you of what you want to talk about. If a lot of words are necessary, consider putting them on a handout instead.
- Learners expect the *key* points to be put on transparency for them. They do not want less important background information to be presented in this way.
- In general, limit the transparency to six or seven lines of text. Make sure it is large enough to be read by someone sitting at the back who has less than perfect vision.
- Colour is not essential, but does add impact and interest.
- Most people think that a horizontal (landscape) orientation is better than a vertical (portrait) orientation; but do not feel constrained by this.
- You can trace pictures directly on to the transparency film.
- For text presentations, settle on a format you like and

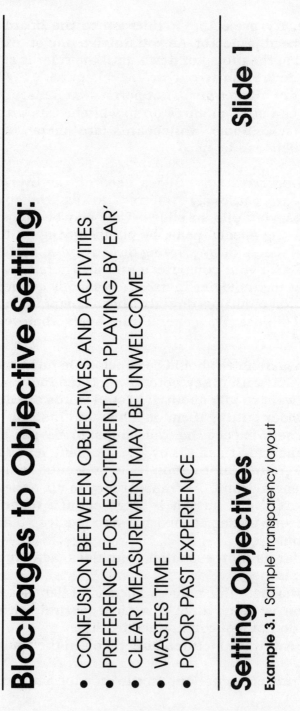

Blockages to Objective Setting:

- CONFUSION BETWEEN OBJECTIVES AND ACTIVITIES
- PREFERENCE FOR EXCITEMENT OF 'PLAYING BY EAR'
- CLEAR MEASUREMENT MAY BE UNWELCOME
- WASTES TIME
- POOR PAST EXPERIENCE

Slide 1

Setting Objectives

Example 3.1 Sample transparency layout

try to keep your transparencies consistent in appearance.
- Number your transparencies as you make them. If generating transparencies by computer, link the numbering to your file name so that you can find the right image when you need it.
- Protect transparencies by using plastic pockets or flip-frame sleeves.
- Always check the spelling. Remember that a computer's spell check will, for example, pass the word 'manger' as well as 'manager'.

Example 3.1 shows a sample layout for an acetate.

Case Studies

The earliest systematic use of case studies in management training is generally credited to the Harvard Business School, with a collection published as long ago as 1954. These involve the detailed examination of actual business cases researched in detail. Students analyse the cases individually, and the classroom discussions tend to produce highly competitive discussion with regard to the quality and accuracy of each person's analysis. However, over the past 40 years, the case study method has been used in many different ways from this, and cases take many forms.

Whatever the format, the purpose of a case study is to enable learners to analyse a situation. This process may involve the use of newly acquired knowledge to consolidate learning or to give a practical illustration of a theoretical framework for analysis. Sometimes a case study is used to stimulate discussion so that, for example, learners are able to compare and contrast their own experiences with the situation described and thus with each other's experiences. As a learning method, case studies are often challenging, stimulating, involving and regarded as highly acceptable by learners.

Case studies may be based on real situations or on

fictional situations. Very often, real situations are modified and fictionalized not only to preserve anonymity but also to focus the case on the particular learning points to be addressed.

Case studies may be useful for the practice of specific skills (e.g. financial analysis; interpreting statistical data; applying motivational models to situations). They are also useful for practising generic skills.

- Analysing
- Problem solving
- Decision making
- Presenting
- Influencing

Additionally, the case method may be a means of promoting teamwork and cooperation.

Although it is possible to provide cases for individual analysis, it is more usual for them to be analysed in small groups. This is usually popular with participants and reduces the stress that less confident learners feel if required to act alone.

How long?

Some case studies may be 40 or 50 pages in length. Although these may be valuable on long postgraduate-level programmes, they are not appropriate for use on short courses. Management time is valuable, and activities should be as time efficient as possible consistent with the intended learning. The designer needs to ask: 'Will a half-page case study bring out the learning points adequately; or is a three-page case really needed?' The shortest case study I use is a single sentence. The longest is four pages. There needs to be sufficient detail to make the situation feel real and believable. On the other hand, long-winded and rambling cases irritate the readers.

On a practical note, people vary enormously in the rate at which they can read and assimilate written material. With a short case, this is seldom a problem. With a longer case, some learners will have finished reading long before others are halfway through. This leads to impatience or embarrassment, and does not produce the desired climate. However, complex situations require reasonably lengthy case material in order for the detail to be introduced properly. It may be better to break a long case into sections to improve its usability, and this process will be discussed later.

Always remember that long case studies need a long time for analysis. Giving a group half an hour to analyse a case which takes them 20 minutes to read will not be appreciated and is a poor use of time.

REAL-LIFE CASES

There are several good reasons why real-life cases may be preferred.

- They are more credible
- They may be easier to produce than invented material
- They can be followed by a 'What actually happened' input

Some learners may attack fictional scenarios: 'That would never happen'; 'Its not realistic'; 'Nobody would make that mistake'. If a case study is based on specific, real incidents, then it is more readily accepted as something that might relate to the learners' own situations.

You can find real-life cases and produce a written document in various ways.

- You may be able to write up a case based on your own experiences and recollections
- You can interview other people and produce a case that details their experiences
- You can find written material

Whenever you write down a case based on either your own or other people's experiences, you should change the names of people and companies involved so as to preserve anonymity. Most case studies look at what went wrong, and the people concerned may not appreciate their actions being scrutinized. Changes should be such that identification is impossible. This is particularly important if the incidents described occurred in the organization in which the training is taking place. Changing Reg White, the warehouse manager into Ron Black, the stores manager, is not enough. Try to resist, however, taking the opportunity to introduce humour into the case by the use of silly names. Calling the characters L. E. Fant, Michael Mouse or Jerry Attrick will simply detract from the learning process.

Written material may come from many sources. It may be possible to buy collections of case material to cover the learning points you want. It is usually more satisfactory to find articles in newspapers or journals which provide the detail you need. Lifting a complete article from a publication will, of course, breach copyright, but taking the facts from an article and writing them in a text of your own is perfectly legal. There are many journals which produce excellent source material regarding such subjects as employment law and health and safety.

Other subjects, such as training and development, suffer from a whitewash treatment in journals. Whereas it is easy to find cases of wonderfully successful training initiatives, nobody ever seems to write up the failures and disasters. With regard to the organization as a whole, there are many books produced which look at successful, and sometimes unsuccessful, organizations, and again factual material can be extracted from them. Business biographies or autobiographies can also provide suitable material.

FICTITIOUS CASES

Fictitious cases may be preferred to real-life cases for a number of reasons. You can, of course, totally control a fictitious case. You can make your characters behave in the way necessary to illustrate the learning points you want, and you can control the environment in which they work. There are no problems with copyright if you prepare your own material. There are three basic strategies to preparing a fictitious case study.

- Create one from your own imagination
- Create one which incorporates some elements from a real incident or a number of incidents, but which is substantially fictitious
- Adapt an existing fictitious case study

BEING CREATIVE

We are all capable of writing creatively. The process comes more easily to some people than it does to others, but the main barrier to creative writing is a self-generated one. We often believe that to be inventive and creative is beyond us because we have not had occasion to put our imaginations to much use for a long time. When we need to generate an appropriate case study, the motivation level is high and should stimulate our creative talents. There are five stages in the creative thinking process.

- Preparation
- Effort
- Incubation
- Insight
- Evaluation

Preparation   We need to be clear about the learning point or points that we intend to cover. We need to have some idea of the time that the case study should take to be analysed. We need to know what will come before and after in the training course.

As an example, suppose we wish to explore the options a supervisor has when giving orders to someone. We may anticipate a tutor-led discussion on this topic that will include requesting, suggesting, requiring, ordering, and so on. To consolidate learning, we may wish to include a case study that will require the course members to consider these options more fully in three syndicate groups.

Perhaps half an hour seems appropriate. How will that time be spent?

- Reading the case – three minutes
- Discussing the case – 12 minutes
- Presenting conclusions – three minutes per syndicate, i.e. nine minutes
- Tutor-led discussion – six minutes

So, we need to write something that will take no more than three minutes to be read by a slow reader. How much can a slow reader absorb in three minutes? This will depend on the educational level of the group, the complexity of what you write and how careful your course members are in their deliberations. However, as a starting point, let us assume that we decide that the maximum length we will let our case be is one page.

Effort This is the stage where we must try hard to generate ideas. Idea production and idea evaluation must be kept separate, as in brainstorming. Do not expect a series of brilliant ideas to flow without any effort; rather, consciously try to associate ideas from as many angles as possible. In our example, we may think of possible scenarios such as the following.

- There has been a disaster due to incorrect procedures – yet the supervisor was sure that the correct orders were given.
- A new supervisor needs to get things done with a variety of people – inexperienced, mature, etc. How should he/she deal with giving instructions?
- An industrial dispute arises because of insensitively given orders.
- A supervisor is failing to achieve targets because subordinates are deliberately (apparently) misinterpreting orders.

Having produced a few ideas, and *jotted them down*, it is usually best to turn our minds to other things. Perhaps a better idea will come later, or a half-formed idea will be stimulated by something we see or hear. This is the stage of incubation.

Incubation It often seems that the unconscious mind can continue to examine the problem for us without much effort, and that our conscious minds can return to the issue refreshed after an interval. Therefore, always allow time for ideas to incubate rather than trying to produce material in one solid slog. If no firm idea seems to be absolutely right, return to the original list and consider the ideas further. Again, jotting thoughts down can be very helpful. Let us return to the list of ideas we produced before.

- *First idea* What kind of disaster? A fatality? Could the case be based around an inquest? What do I know about inquests? Not much. Anyway, it's a bit morbid. What about a financial disaster? Or perhaps an opening ceremony going wrong? Do I have experience of organizing an opening ceremony? Yes. Did anything go wrong? Yes – not much, but it could have been a lot worse.
- *Second idea* What kind of thing? Perhaps setting up a training room for an important visitor. Or it could be a production or sales or administration situation. But the trainees from sales won't like a production situation, and vice versa. Could I generate an administrative example which would suit all of them? Or should I set the scene in an alien environment for all of them, such as in a hotel?
- *Third idea* What kind of dispute? A grievance, or a strike? Will they immediately take sides with the supervisor even if the orders were badly given?
- *Fourth idea* Again, in what area? Production or sales? Or how about distribution? It's a more relevant scenario than some of the others.

Insight Sometimes, during the mulling over process, there will be the flash of insight that says 'Yes, that would work!' More often, it will be a gradual warming to an idea, perhaps accompanied by a growing confidence. Bouncing possibilities off colleagues often clarifies thinking at this point. Some people find the mind-mapping technique extremely useful when trying to clarify complex situations (Buzan, 1989).

Evaluation   Now all the ideas previously considered must be returned to and examined, even if the 'insight' stage has left a clear favourite.

- *First idea*   Yes, a definite possibility.
- *Second idea*   Possible, but on reflection, it seems somewhat unexciting. Hold.
- *Third idea*   Not a good idea. Too many pitfalls. Reject.
- *Fourth idea*   Possible, but care would be needed in the writing to make it equally relevant to them all. Hold.

Okay. We have now provisionally selected an idea – the First idea. However, we have not totally rejected two of the others because they could work. In due course, we may find that our chosen idea does not work out well, and it is comforting to have something in reserve. Some trainers keep an ideas file to be referred to when a different learning need arises. An idea rejected for this problem might well be useful for another problem.

WRITING THE CASE

Having settled on an idea, we must now actually start writing. Before we do, let us remind ourselves of what we want to get out of the case.

- We want to stimulate the learners to discuss various ways of giving instructions so as clarify when the various styles are appropriate and when they are not.

It would be possible to develop this aim into precise behavioural objectives if this were required but, as the content of the discussion will be different for each group, it is often more honest to accept that the learning outcomes are not totally predictable from a case study. If you want to be precise about the outcomes, it is often easier to write the objectives after the case has been written. This is what most trainers actually do, even though few of us admit it.

Developing the plot   Jot down some rough notes as to how the case can develop. Make notes for yourself as you go along, including points on which you have yet to decide:

A supervisor (*male, female, or unstated? Named?*) is tasked with organizing an opening ceremony for a new warehouse or office block. *This instruction could either be given well or be given badly.*

The supervisor has to work through other people (*reflect the types of people found in the organization*) to get the various tasks done. Things to be organized could include, for example:

- catering
- photographer
- flagpoles
- inviting guests (*royalty, chairman or chairwoman, celebrity?*)
- furniture
- transport

Show four or five different styles of instruction. This could relate to the previous tutor input very directly.

Some aspects go well, some go badly. Some remedial action is called for. *This could be included, or it could be the basis for the group to make decisions about.*

Now actually start writing. Word processors are marvellous for this kind of activity as they allow for continuous revision. However, to reduce your inhibitions, label the document 'draft'. Example 3.2 shows a draft case outline.

Once the first draft is finished, leave it. Put it away and forget about it for a few days. Then re-read it. Amend it, develop it, rework it as necessary until a usable case study has been produced. Then, as with all other

Pat Jenkins felt nervous as she approached the door of Clive Senior, the northern regional manager. She knocked lightly on the mahogany door. 'Come in,' bellowed Clive. 'Nice to see you, Pat. I'm off to Paris in a few minutes, so I'll get straight to the point. As you know, the builders will be finishing the new office block in a few days time. Lady Barwell will be visiting this site at the end of next week, and Sir Giles, the company chairman, has asked her to perform an opening ceremony for us. I'm sorry to drop this on you, but I won't be back until the day itself, so I'd like you to organize everything . . .

Example 3.2 Draft case outline

material, try it out. If possible, use the case with a group you know well. After the course, ask them for feedback. Evaluate the activity in isolation and in the wider context of the course.

Games and Exercises

There is a lot of confusion between concepts such as 'games and exercises' when used in a training context. For the sake of clarity, therefore, let us first look at some key characteristics.

Games

- are competitive
- involve scoring or racing to produce winners
- have rules
- have participants – the players

Exercises

- do not have roles
- maintain objectivity
- may be individual or group

- are often about analysing situations that have been described rather than experienced

GAMES

Games are introduced into training events for a number of reasons. One of the main benefits of using games is that they are (usually) fun. Being given a task to accomplish very quickly in competition with others produces a buzz of excitement and energy that participants find invigorating. The purpose of the game will often be to provide an opportunity to look at teamwork, leadership, organization or planning. The value of the game is in the lessons that can be drawn from the processes that took place during the activity, so that participants gain insight into the principles under consideration or into their own behaviour.

There are some dangers with the use of games.

- Some people reject them as childish, and either do not participate at all or do so without commitment
- Some people get so involved with the game that they may get upset about losing or believe that having won they have nothing to learn
- The lessons to be learned from the way in which the game went may be difficult to translate into a back-at-work model
- Some games have tricks built into them that can cause resentment
- Some games are so widely used that there is a chance that participants will have experienced them before
- Some trainers use the games without ensuring that the appropriate learning takes place. Everyone has a good time, but that's all

EXERCISES

In an exercise, participants remain themselves. They analyse and discuss situations which may be given to them in a variety of ways. Exercises can be cooperative, and may be open-ended. They may be brief, or fairly extensive. Types of exercise include the following.

- Case study
- Problem solving
- Task completion
- Review of participants' experiences
- Brainstorming

As before, any exercise should be used with specific purposes in mind. During a long training course, as many different kinds of exercise as possible should be used to help maintain interest.

Case study exercises come in many different forms, and are dealt with separately.

Problem solving exercises are often used to illustrate the necessity of teamwork or sharing of information or, indeed, to look at the process of problem solving itself.

Task-completion exercises will often be used in general management or team building courses as a vehicle for looking at leadership or the process of task accomplishment. They need not be competitive, but often small groups work in parallel so that everyone is involved and differences in approach can be studied.

Reviews of participants' experience can be extremely effective if not used too often. This type of exercise may start with 'Think of the worst training event that you ever attended. Why was it so bad?', and so on.

Brainstorming approaches can be useful to get ideas out very fast followed by discussion – for example, 'In groups of three or four, list at least 20 types of insurance policy'.

Whatever type of exercise is used, timing is often crucial – too little, and some of the value is lost; too much, and the course begins to drag. Be prepared to modify timings with experience.

Role Playing

Role playing is one of the oldest techniques devised to assist learners by direct experience in a simulated setting. Role playing is often very helpful in working on problems in a way that produces graphic illustrations of effective or ineffective behaviour which the participants have generated for themselves. They have not simply observed someone else act out a situation, as they do when they watch a dramatized training video, but they have had to put effort, and perhaps emotion, into the process.

Role play ought to be an opportunity to practise behaviours in a risk-free, safe setting. This is not automatically the case, and people can get upset if a role play gets out of hand. Participants can get carried away with the situation, or use it to score points in an aggressive manner. For some people the role play method can be quite abhorrent, while others relish the chance to demonstrate their dramatic skills.

STARTING ROLE PLAYING

In a role play, the trainer provides a clear definition of the situation in as much detail as is necessary. Often a very brief description will suffice, but some role-play briefs can be quite lengthy. Individuals are selected or volunteer to be characters to play the various roles in acting out the situations. They may be briefed publicly or privately. The brief may be verbal or written, or a mixture. Time to prepare may be allowed. The drama may take place with or without part of the group as an audience. Some people find role playing in front of a large audience extremely stressful, and it is often best to, leave this to volunteers.

Role plays can be left open-ended or subject to strict time limits. Sometimes they are interrupted for discussion after interesting points have emerged. They may or may not be recorded. In any event, the process must be analysed and discussed on completion so that learning points are fully absorbed.

USES OF ROLE PLAY

Role play can be used to:

- illustrate clearly a feature of some specific behaviour in a lively and direct way. This can include features of non-verbal behaviour that cannot be clearly illustrated otherwise
- increase the involvement of the group; effort is required from them and a well-performed role play leads to a feeling of accomplishment
- provide a common experience for the group to discuss
- practise specific behavioural skills, such as inter-viewing, chairing a meeting or greeting customers
- help people understand a situation from the viewpoint of others – having to play the part of someone who has the opposite role to that usually performed in real life often produces a significant increase in empathy and understanding; for example, a manager who plays the role of a union representative defending a colleague from dismissal may achieve far more insight in this way than from simply discussing the situation
- give insight into their own behaviour and the effect this has on others
- make possible experimentation in a no-risk setting; Participants can try tactics that are new to them, or employ alternative behaviours to evaluate their effec-tiveness

POINTS TO WATCH

- It is usually best to keep written descriptions as brief as possible. Very long, detailed scenarios are difficult for people to memorize and items which have been inserted for background can end up dominating the discussion.
- Sometimes it is better for the trainer to choose partici-

pants, sometimes to call for volunteers. You should aim to avoid anyone trying to perform a role play which is beyond him or her. The participant may feel humiliated or inadequate, or may rubbish the exercise, with reactions like 'It's not real', 'The brief was unclear' or 'I would never do that'.

- Avoid boss–subordinate pairings unless you have a good reason for them.
- Watching too many role plays one after the other can become boring for audiences.
- Beware the over-exuberant character who turns your description of a slightly disgruntled customer into a raving monster.
- People find it hard to play characters of a different age group or of the opposite gender. It is often possible to write roles which allow participants to project themselves into the situation. Rather than 'You are a 56-year-old transport manager named Norman who wants to tell Mandy, the 19-year-old typist, to cut down on private telephone calls', try 'You are a manager who has decided to tell a subordinate to cut down on private telephone calls'.
- If it is easier to use names, try to reflect the organization's gender and cultural mix in the role plays. But take care not to stereotype.
- It is the trainer's responsibility to protect participants from role plays which get out of hand.
- It is sometimes possible to create role plays on the spot from incidents described by course members. For instance, members of the group may be asked to describe situations which they have found difficult to handle. One or two of these may then be acted out to determine the best way to resolve the problems described.
- Debrief. Ensure that the mistakes made by the role character are seen as such, not as those of the person playing that character. Role plays often stimulate conflict. If the debriefing does not allow the participants

to discard their roles, then you may have created tensions and animosities between course members.

- Review what happened. Make sure that anyone who has been designated as an observer is allowed to report what she or he has observed. In leading the discussion:
  a. determine what happened
  b. identify what went well
  c. explore the way in which the situation developed and the reasons the role players behaved as they did
  d. discuss how the situation might be better handled or how real situations differ
- When the situation is appropriate, allow a second go to get it right.

Two role-play briefs are shown in example 3.3.

As previously mentioned, you can also ask people to create their own role plays. Although this may take more time and effort, the results may be much more relevant and therefore more effective. However, people do vary in their ability to prepare such activities, so having back-up material is helpful. I also find it helps to give them forms to complete as they go along, such as the set shown in example 3.4.

Handouts

Most kinds of training benefit from the provision of appropriate reference material. It may serve two main purposes. First, it may provide the learner with a reminder of what has been put across on the course. Some of the learners will read the material immediately, others may not. In many cases what will happen is that the folder will be put on a shelf, but in weeks or months to come it will be referred to as a particular need arises. Handouts should not replace the process of note taking, which aids memory, but ensure that everyone has a full and accurate version of the information. A second purpose of handout material is to give more depth of coverage on certain

ROLE-PLAY BRIEF – A

You are a storekeeper, Lee Martin.

You are conscientious in your duties. Your insistence on following procedures does not always make you popular; but it's your job to ensure that the rules are complied with. Recently, you have been subject to considerable pressure because you have refused to shortcut the rules. If the procedure requires a manager's signature before you release a part, then a telephone call is simply not good enough. If everyone else followed the rules, you would have few problems. Apart, of course, from the new computerized systems.

Operating the system is no problem, unless you make a mistake. Then it is a real performance to correct it. Once or twice a week you have to ask Rachel from accounts to sort out problems. She used to help willingly, but now her boss is getting funny about letting her come to the stores so often – probably because she spends half an hour chatting to Wayne in the yard on the way back.

One grumble you have is that you used to get help to keep the stores clean and tidy, but now you have to do it all yourself. It isn't your top priority.

ROLE-PLAY BRIEF – B

You are preparing to appraise a storekeeper, Lee Martin.

Lee is conscientious in his duties. However, his insistence on following procedures makes him unpopular. On one recent occasion, Lee refused to release a part because the system had not been followed correctly, and this led to some avoidable downtime.

Lee is having trouble learning the new computerized system. He has had a lot of help from accounts, but they have other things to do.

One matter you wish to tackle is housekeeping. Remind Lee of the importance of housekeeping. You expect he will harp on about the time when there was more staff, but there is nothing you can do about staffing levels.

Example 3.3 Role-play briefs

Disciplinary exercise

Form A

Think about the people for whom you are responsible. Select someone who has one major or several minor weaknesses which need to be addressed in order to improve performance and who has not responded to subtle indications. If necessary, exaggerate the problem(s) or combine a few individuals' faults.

1. Prepare an interviewer's brief – as if you were looking at the situation from outside and were briefing yourself for the encounter. Use a fictitious name, please. Do this on form B. Form B will be given to someone else who will prepare and conduct the interview.

2. You will play the character described.

Form B: Interviewer's brief

Your name is .... (*use a fictitious name*)

Your present position is:

.... in .... department

The interviewee's name is: .... (*use a fictitious name*)

He/she has been employed for ....

He/she works as a ....

His/her performance is:

Example 3.4 Self-generated role play

points. It may not be a good use of time to go into a lot of background information on a course, but the handout material can do so. Case examples can be given for the learner to read about.

When preparing a training session you will be collecting a lot of information about the subject in question.

Writing a handout is a good way of clarifying your own understanding and also helps with the structure of the input. As you write the handout you can spot key points which will form the basis of a visual aid. Writing these in a handout will enable you to say yes to the question 'Is this in a handout?' which frequently crops up when information is displayed on a visual aid.

It is often tempting to shortcut the process of writing handouts by using existing material, perhaps written by someone else for another purpose. This can result in the embarrassment of not being able to explain part of the text, or issuing something that directly contradicts what you have been saying. It is all too easy to find yourself talking about the four stages of problem solving and issuing a handout which contains the five stages of problem solving. You will lose credibility very quickly if you do this.

How long and detailed the handouts should be depends on your learners and their needs. Detailed and lengthy handouts will often not be read, and some trainers like to give handouts which are essentially a series of bullet points. I personally prefer to issue handouts which are fairly full because I have had feedback from some learners who say they prefer this.

Handouts can be enlivened by pictures and diagrams (example 3.5) and can be made as lively or as serious as is appropriate.

CODING

At first, you will remember every handout you write. Every exercise, case study and role play will be clearly recalled. After a year or two, though, you may find that it takes hours to find a particular document. Questions such as 'What course is the handout on leadership in?', 'What role plays have we got?' Have we any good exercises on planning?' can become difficult to answer. Modern word processors help immensely, but can be rendered much less effective by the absence of a usable coding system.

Securing agreement

When dealing with complaints, we should normally aim to achieve a settlement which both parties regard as fair and which brings an end to the complaint. We all have defensive emotional reactions which are basic and strong, and which tend to make us defend a position when a complaint is lodged to turn it to our own advantage.

Normally, a complaint is valuable feedback that something has gone wrong. We should overcome our instincts and thank the person who brings a complaint

Example 3.5 Part of a handout with pictures

It is sensible to use the same system for the paper copies as for the word processing files. There are many possibilities. One simple one is:

Handouts: H1, H2, H3, etc.
Case studies: CS1, CS2, CS3, etc.
Exercises: E1, E2, E3, etc.

Another possibility is to add a second code to indicate contents:

H1qual   (quality)
H2lead   (leadership)
H3safe   (safety)
H4safe   (safety)
H5cust   (customer care)

Some people like to code by course:

EM1–1   (electrical maintenance, module one, document one)

EM1–2   (electrical maintenance, module one, document two)

EM1–3   (electrical maintenance, module one, document three)

EM2–1   (electrical maintenance, module two, document one)

MM4–2   (mechanical maintenance, module four, document two)

Whatever coding System is adopted, it will also be necessary to have a procedure for revising and updating material. This is particularly important where more than one trainer is involved. If an agreed procedure is not in place, then it is easy to end up with two or three versions of the same handout title with the same code.

A coding system is also invaluable when assembling material for printing or photocopying. Instead of working to a list of titles, the person doing this works with a list of codes. This is much easier and makes checking quicker.

Summary

This chapter has dealt with the preparation of various kinds of training materials. There are many other kinds of training material of such as videos and computer-based learning systems, that have not dealt with here. These are specialized disciplines that require in-depth study, but with which many trainers will never become involved. Instead, I have concentrated on the most widely used technologies and activities. The production of materials has been considered under the following headings.

• Visual aids
• Case studies
• Games and exercises
• Role playing

- Handouts

Inevitably, the topics of design and production have over-lapped. The processes of preparation include creative thinking as well as applying a systematic and disciplined approach. What is sometimes overlooked is that these processes which lead to good-quality training materials also lead to thorough understanding of the topic in the trainer. The best way for a trainer to prepare for the delivery of a training event is to write and produce the materials for himself or herself. This often, of course, requires background reading, investigation and analysis. This is how a real depth of expertise is developed which is apparent in what the trainer says as well as in the material that he or she has produced.

ACTIVITIES

1   Preparing overhead projection slides

Introduction   A simple activity in which learners are required to design and produce a mainly pictorial over-head slide.

Aims   To allow practice of overhead slide production and to emphasize the importance of good visual design.

Methods   In pairs or singly, learners are asked to design and produce an opening slide for an imaginary presentation. You might choose one of the following topics.

- My favourite television programme
- A sporting event
- A day in the country
- It's show time!

Participants should be provided with whatever materials are considered appropriate (e.g. acetates, pens) and may be encouraged to trace pictures out of magazines or newspapers. Alternatively, computer-based graphics packages can be used. The slides are displayed and judged by the whole group on whichever of the following criteria are deemed appropriate.

- Impact
- Relevance
- Use of colour
- Artistic merit
- Creativity

Marks out of five may be given, and discussion generated as to the importance of various aspects of slide design.

Timing   About 30 minutes to design and produce a slide. Allow a further three or four minutes for display and judging of each slide, followed by approximately 15 minutes for discussion.

2   Structuring a presentation

Introduction   Learners are given a news report and asked to produce a slide showing how they would structure a presentation about that news. Reports may be torn from a newspaper. Alternatively, use the fictitious article 'Warning shot' which appears below.

Aims   To give learners the opportunity to decide how to structure a presentation.

Method   Split the group into pairs or triads. Provide a newspaper article of suitable length and interest. Brief them to produce a plan of how they would structure a five-minute presentation about the report given. It may be useful to specify that the presentation should contain, for example, five slides.

Timings   Twenty minutes to prepare, and about five minutes to view and discuss each plan.

Warning shot

The American vice-president, Harvey Hopkins, was involved in an incident in which Russian security police accompanying him fired a warning shot at a motorist. Mr Hopkins was being escorted in a six-car motorcade which was approaching the Kremlin when a motorist cut across the middle of the convoy and appeared to be about to pull alongside the car containing the vice-president.

A detective in the car behind produced a handgun and fired a single shot over the roof of the intruding car, believed to be a Lada, which then veered away. Police did not pursue the vehicle, and the official view is that the motorist had simply failed to appreciate the nature of the convoy.

A spokesman for the vice-presidential party stated: 'We do not believe there was ever any danger to the vice-president. This is the sort of incident that could happen anywhere, and we were very pleased with the firm and decisive way in which the possible threat was dealt with by the Russian escort.'

The vice-president is in Moscow on an official goodwill visit lasting ten days. It is not the first time he has been involved in a security scare. Last year, whilst in France for a meeting with European industrialists, a young woman was arrested attempting to enter his hotel carrying a concealed sub-machine-gun. She later claimed to be a member of an extremist ecological group which blames the USA for much of the destruction of the world's rain forests.

In a more recent incident, a bomb was discovered in a Detroit conference centre three days before Mr Hopkins was due to speak there. Although several groups subsequently claimed responsibility for the bomb, police feel that it was most likely that an individual with a grudge had made and planted the device. No arrests have yet been made.

The recent increase in attempts to kill senior American politicians has alarmed the administration. It calls into question the proposed fact-finding tour of African states by a group of senators and congressmen scheduled for next year. One White House spokesman is reported to have said that the only way the trip would go ahead was in 'armoured cars escorted by helicopter gunships'.

3 Create a game

Introduction   This activity should follow on from input and discussion about the design process.

Aims   To give the opportunity to be creative in the design of an activity.

Method   Divide the group into pairs (or threes for a large group) and issue the following instructions.

> During the next 30 minutes you must create a game which people from the other groups will play. The game should last about five minutes. Use only materials readily to hand (e.g. paper, coins, etc.). The game must produce a clear winner, and should have the objective of enabling players to demonstrate their creativity. Please do not simply use a game you have already played, but be creative in the design process.

Timings   Thirty minutes to prepare, and about ten minutes to set up and run each activity. Also allow some time to discuss the difficulties of designing such an activity in such a short time, the difficulty of predicting time requirements, and other learning points as appropriate.

4 Role play case study

Jenny's solo run

Jenny had been rather nervous about running the negotiating skills course on her own for the first time. Still, she had thought, she had helped Sue run it twice before and it had always gone well. All the material was prepared to a high standard. 'Apart from some input at the beginning, it runs itself', Sue had said.

It had been a reasonable morning, thought Jenny. No mistakes with the input and discussions, and they had all enjoyed the video. Now she would get the role play exercise going, and that would provide a good afternoon's session. Just as she had seen Sue do, Jenny divided the course into two groups and issued the role briefings. The role play was based around an industrial relations scenario, with one group playing the management team and one playing a trade union team. There were five people in each team. After she had issued the briefings, she sent the two teams away to prepare for the next half hour. She would run the exercise just like Sue did, with no interference and without commenting until the end.

At the end of the preparation time, Jenny sent the management team back into the training room first to prepare for the negotiation. The union team, however, would not go back. Graham, a mid-thirties production manager, had been elected as the 'senior shop steward' by his group. He insisted that the management team should come and ask them politely to attend the meeting. Jenny went along with this, but the management side would not comply! It took her nearly ten minutes of persuasion to get Graham to lead his team back to the training room.

When they arrived back, the management team was seated behind a row of tables at the far end of the room. There were no other chairs left in the room for the union team to use. Another five minutes was wasted sorting that difficulty out.

When, at last, the negotiations actually started, Jenny was horrified by Graham's behaviour. He shouted and swore. He banged the table with his fist. At one point it looked as if he would actually throw the table over. Jenny was not the only one who was horrified. The management team had appointed Jonathan, a young management trainee from accounts, as their lead negotiator. He was no match for Graham and quickly caved in to most of Graham's demands. Some of Jonathan's team objected to Graham's tactics. 'It's not fair,' said Alison. 'This is supposed to be a learning experience, not a slanging match.' Graham was in victorious mood, however, and simply stood his ground with the baying support of two of his 'union' partners. The other two, however, had not said a word. Eventually, one of them, Paul from management services, announced quietly that he had 'had enough of this nonsense' and left the room. He was closely followed by his colleague.

By now Jonathan had completely withdrawn and was looking deeply upset. Alison was trying to counsel him while the other three team members continued to argue with Graham and his two cronies that the negotiation should start again. Alison glared across at Jenny. 'Do something!' she hissed.

What should Jenny do now? What should she have done in the first place?

5 Role-play design exercise

Introduction A design exercise in which people are asked to create a role play which is then tried out.

Aims To give the opportunity to create a role-play exercise, and to see how it works in practice.

Method Divide the group into threes and issue the following instructions (adapted as necessary).

During the next 45 minutes you must create a role play which people from the other groups will perform. The role play should last about ten minutes and should involve two or three people. The role play should have the objective of allowing participants to practise some skill or behaviour that is relevant to their role at work. For example, dealing with a disciplinary problem, coping with a difficult telephone call from a customer or asking someone to stop disrupting a course. Please do not simply use a role play you are already familiar with, but be creative in the design process.

Once prepared, groups take it in turns to brief participants from another group to perform the role play. They also analyse the learning points from the role play performance, and debrief as necessary. The qualities and limitations of the role play design are then discussed and learning points extracted.

Timings About 45 minutes preparation of the role plays followed by a further 20 minutes per group for the performances and performance reviews. Allow a total of around 30 minutes for the design considerations to be discussed.

FURTHER READING

BACIE 1970: *Bacie Case Studies* London: BACIE.

Buzan, T. 1989: *Use Your Head* (revised edn). London: BBC Books.

Rae, L. 1995: *Techniques of Training* (3rd edn). Aldershot: Gower.

Stuart, C. 1988: *Effective Speaking*. London: Pan.

Townsend, J. 1993: *The Instructor's Pocketbook* (6th edn). London: Management Pocketbooks.

4

Delivery Skills

The devil's name is Dullness.
> **Robert E. Lee**, Chambers Book of Quotations

Presentation Techniques

Good training and good presenting are not the same thing. It is possible to find excellent trainers who say that they never give a presentation as such. Equally, some excellent presenters are not good trainers. Presenting information is only one aspect of training. None the less, it is a very important aspect because a presentation:

- is an effective way of giving information to a group
- may be necessary to gain commitment from a management team
- is how some people judge a trainer's competence
- can be useful to summarize learning points

Delivering a presentation is a skill that people have to learn. Although it is true that some people find it easier than others, everyone is capable of learning presentation techniques to some degree. There are points of technique to be learned and practised, and all of us must evolve ways of presenting which suit our particular personalities. There is no single right way to deliver a presentation in a training context. A good trainer will employ a range of styles that will vary according to the particular combination of subject matter, audience and other circumstances that he or she may encounter on different occasions.

CONFIDENCE

For many people, lack of confidence is the biggest single obstacle to delivering an effective presentation. This leads to nervousness and anxiety, and hence to a stilted and awkward performance. Thus, the individual becomes convinced that he or she is no good at giving presentations, and avoids doing them. This leads to a negative cycle (example 4.1), which inhibits improvement. It is therefore necessary to break this cycle to increase confidence.

Lack of confidence has three causes.

- Fear of looking foolish
- Fear of the audience's reaction
- Fear of drying up

Fear of looking foolish   The fear that many of us experience when standing in front of a group can be intense. If we are not used to it, the psychological pressure of having people staring at us can be quite incapacitating. First, it can be reduced by thinking about what clothes you will wear and your appearance in general. This is often easier

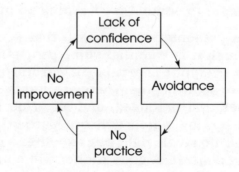

Example 4.1 A negative cycle

for men to get right because there is less choice. Usually, a conventional suit, shirt and tie will be appropriate, but more casual clothing may the right choice in some situations. Some experienced trainers deliberately wear loud ties to achieve impact. But if you are inexperienced, worrying about the possible reaction to any aspect of your appearance will add anxiety – so stick to a safe shirt and tie combination. Some audiences can react against too much style, so think about whether they would admire a designer suit or classify you as a poser. I recall one trainer who always dressed very smartly but who was described by a member of his audience as looking like 'a head waiter in an Italian restaurant'. Jewellery and cologne may build empathy with one audience but create alienation with the next. Think about your appearance in relation to the audience concerned.

Women often have greater difficulty in deciding what to wear because of the wider range available to them. As for men, a smart, conventional, appearance is the safest bet. Women may also feel additional pressure because of the way some men stare at them. If you wish to reduce this pressure, avoid clothes that draw attention to your body. Short skirts, semi-transparent blouses or plunging necklines may not only put pressure on you but may also detract from your credibility. A very youthful style of dress or hairstyle can also reduce your credibility, as can excessive jewellery or make-up. Again, think about your appearance in relation to your audience.

Providing you have thought about it, you will probably get your appearance near enough right for the audience not to be affected by it and for you to feel psychologically comfortable. Make sure that you will be physically comfortable as well by avoiding new shoes, tight collars, etc. Wear clothes that will be warm enough but not uncomfortably hot. Jackets are easy and quick to take off or put on; sweaters are not.

Having thought about appearance, the second thing to think about is starting the presentation. This is the most stressful part of any event. Reduce the pressure on yourself by having a visual aid ready for use after the opening minute or two. As the overhead projector is switched on, the audience's eyes will turn from you on to the screen. You will probably feel the tension diminish, and as you relax you will be able to talk more fluently.

Third, remember that you don't have to be perfect. Your audience will forgive occasional stumblings and other signs of nerves. They too will have a fear of speaking to groups or will remember what it was like before they became experienced.

Finally, this fear will diminish with practice. Force yourself to 'stand and deliver' a few times and get beyond the feelings of fear and into the feelings of accomplishment and satisfaction that can come from this activity.

Fear of the audience's reaction They are there to learn, and if they think you know what you are talking about they will respond naturally to your input. Try to anticipate their attitude. If you have pitched your presentation to their needs, then their reaction is likely to be appreciative and encouraging. Reduce your anxiety about the audience by meeting them in advance, if you can. Again, experience will reduce your fear of audiences. Most of them are kind and friendly.

Fear of drying up Thorough preparation is the key. You know your subject and you know you know it. Reduce the fear by having notes so that you can remind yourself of what you were going to say. How to prepare notes will be dealt with later in this section, but it is important to stress that you must prepare your own notes. Using somebody else's notes does not commit the presentation to memory in the same way. Timing of an input session is difficult, so keep it flexible by having some material which can be left out if time is short or included if there is ample time.

PREPARATION

Before you can begin to prepare a presentation, it is necessary to ask yourself a series of questions:

- What is the purpose of the presentation?
- Who is the audience?
- What are the circumstances?

The purpose There are three categories into which the purpose of most presentations falls.

- Communicating information
- Making a proposition
- Inspiring and motivating

In a training context, the presentation may serve all three of these purposes simultaneously. For example, the trainer may want to:

- Outline an appraisal scheme
- Persuade the audience to support the concept
- Generate enthusiasm for the introduction of the scheme

The commonest purpose of the trainer's presentation is to impart knowledge. When this is the case, it is usually simple to generate a concise overall objective statement, such as 'By the end of the presentation, the members of the audience will be able to list the four main stages in the selection and purchase of a new photocopier'. If more than one purpose is being served, then obviously more than objective statement must be generated.

The audience The members of the audience will influence the presentation in several ways. Before beginning to prepare, it is necessary to consider the following questions.

- Who will be present?
- How many will be present?
- What is the extent of their existing knowledge?

- What will be of interest to them?
- What attitudes, preconceptions or expectations will they bring with them?

The presentation should be pitched as accurately as possible for the audience. Explaining things at too elementary a level will leave the audience bored and frustrated; assuming they know more than they actually do can result in their losing the thread and failing to absorb the message. Either way, the audience will become irritated and will resent your lack of consideration for them. However, it is not always possible to gain accurate information about the audience. When it is, the audience may be found to be very mixed in terms of existing expertise, age, education and so on. In this case, consider whether it is possible to reorganize the presentation to overcome these problems. It may be possible to provide background information for those that need it in advance. Otherwise, acknowledge the problem to the audience. Explain that some of them may find some aspects rather elementary and ask for their forbearance. Plan to use their knowledge to support your presentation if possible.

The circumstances Other factors that have to be taken into account at this stage are the general and specific circumstances in which you will be operating.

- The venue
- Equipment
- The time available
- The context

You may have a wide choice of venue, or you may have none. You need to know the size of the room, the furniture, position of power points and other practical considerations. If they are not ideal, can a better venue be found, or must you make do come what may?

You may have access to the full range of modern audio-visual equipment or none at all. You must know what is available and select the appropriate aids for your purpose.

Ideally, you should have as much time as you need to put across your message and no more. In practice, you may be allocated a very specific time slot and have to make the best use of it. We often underestimate the time needed to put across a complex message, so if time is limited the message may have to be simplified.

The context in which a presentation is delivered is important. Is it at the start of the day with a group who are new to each other, or is it the fourth item in a crowded agenda? Are you being judged against others making similar presentations, or will they only see yours? Are you bringing good news that will be eagerly anticipated, or bad news that will provoke hostility? Only when all these questions have been addressed can the presenter move on to the detailed preparation, the planning, of the presentation.

PLANNING

There are various methods that people use to plan a presentation. One popular way is to jot down key words or phrases to cover all the points that might be included in the presentation. At all times, the objective of the presentation should be kept in mind. At this stage, do not worry about sequence or timing.

A good presentation, like a good story, has a beginning, a middle and an end.

- Introduction
- Development
- Conclusion

Paradoxically, the introduction is best prepared after the other material. This is because the introduction will outline the content of the development section, and so this must be prepared first. To do this, the points already noted down must be grouped under appropriate headings. Three or four major sections should evolve, and as you work a theme will probably suggest itself. Some of the points will fit best into the introduction or conclusion sections. Others may not fit well anywhere. Perhaps the section headings need to be revised, or maybe the points should be dropped from the presentation altogether. Do not expect to be able to arrive at a satisfactory plan in one go. If you get stuck or confused, leave it. Do something else for a while and let your mind clear. Often, when you return to the problem, things will fall into place more readily.

Once you have decided upon the content, the next stage is to work out a logical sequence and timings. The sequence will depend on the nature of the content. Sometimes it will be obvious (for example, historical development); sometimes less so. It may not even be important. Try different ideas until it feels right. Timing can be achieved either by speaking aloud what you intend to say, and noting the time taken, or by making the material fit the time you decide. Your broad outline may look like example 4.2.

Then prepare your notes. Try not to write a speech; rather write down key words or phrases to remind you of what you wish to say. Note down the points at which you might use a visual aid. Some people like to use cards as prompts; others are happier using a flat sheet of paper. Try different approaches until you settle on one which you are happy with. Your notes may look something like example 4.3.

Time available: 20 minutes
Introduction: 2 minutes (10%)
Development:
  Historical background: 4 minutes (20%)
  Recent developments: 5 minutes (25%)
  Case examples: 6 minutes (30%)
Conclusion: 3 minutes (15%)

Example 4.2 Outline timing for a presentation

```
Welcome
Introduction  - Self
              - Topic (equal opportunity policy)
              - Reason for presentation and its scope
                                                2 minutes


OHP1:  'The law'
       Key points - Sex Discrimination Act
                  - Equal Pay Act
                  - Race Relations Act
                                                5 minutes


OHP2:  'Why do we need a policy?'
       Key points - Codes of practice
                  - Consistency
                  - Moral arguments
                                                6 minutes

and so on.
```

Example 4.3 Notes for a presentation

REHEARSAL AND PRACTICE

A rehearsal is an important element in the preparation of a presentation. If possible, use the actual venue where your presentation will be delivered. One of the key purposes of the rehearsal is to check the timing. Find out if your time estimates are near the mark or way off. Your timings need not be absolutely precise; remember that an audience slows you down.

Even if you do not rehearse standing in front of an empty room, practise what you are going to say by using your notes as triggers. This can be done at home, and you can ask friends or relatives to give their reactions. Rehearse key points. If you are going to move around, practise this too, so that your movement looks purposeful and authoritative, instead of random and pointless. If you are using visual aids, practise their use as well. Knowing how to switch the projector on before you appear in front of the audience may sound obvious, but you will probably be able to remember an occasion when the presenter had to call for assistance!

Well before the day, decide what you are going to wear. Remember to choose clothes that make you feel both comfortable and confident. Make sure that your chosen outfit is clean and presentable.

DELIVERING A PRESENTATION

It is not really possible to learn much about the delivery of a presentation by reading about it, so I will be brief.

Project enthusiasm   Many of the most popular presenters would fail an assessment from a 'purist' expert in presentation techniques. They are popular because they project energy, enthusiasm and belief into their sessions. This projection comes across in the voice, posture, gestures, eyes and body movement. I would far rather listen to an enthusiast with poor visual aids than to someone who looked bored and tired with perfect visual aids. Of course, if you get both right . . .

Eye contact   Look at your audience from the beginning. Smile at them. Do not, however, fix on one friendly face, but rather scan the audience. This creates empathy, and also lets you read their reaction to what you are saying.

Voice   You have to speak loudly without shouting. This takes practice, but it can be learned. You can also vary the volume, speaking up to add emphasis or dropping to a near whisper to signify the sharing of a secret. Also, you should vary your speed of delivery and the pitch of your voice. Stuart 1988 deals with these matters particularly well.

Using an overhead projector   Thoroughly familiarize yourself with how the projector works. There are only a few controls.

All projectors have:

- an on/off switch
- a focus knob, which raises or lowers the 'head' on the upright post
- a mirror, which can be angled to place the image on the screen

Some also have:

- a second on/off switch
- a spare bulb lever – this physically moves the spare bulb into place
- an intensity switch usually next to the on/off switch
- a 'fringe colouration eliminator knob'. This is used to minimize the orange or blue fringe sometimes found at the edge of the screen. Overhead projectors without such a device do not seem to suffer from this effect

To project an overhead slide first ensure that the mirror is raised, otherwise heat rapidly builds up within the head and can cause damage. Then simply place it on the stage glass (or 'platen') and switch on. Focus the image with the focus knob and align the image on the screen by moving the mirror up and down. To alter the size of the image, you must alter the distance between the screen and the projector by moving one or the other. A typical distance between projector and screen will be two metres, and this should be considered when selecting a training room. In general, the projector should be placed as far away from direct sunlight as possible.

You can point to something on the slide either by using a pointer on the screen or by placing a pen or pencil on the slide as it rests on the stage glass of the projector. The latter method is considered by some to be more professional, but it really does not matter.

The projector should be switched off when not in use. Never leave a slide up after you have moved on in the session, and never leave the projector beaming out white light. It draws the eye and is a distraction. Some people insist that the projector should be switched off while you change slides, but it is not really necessary.

Do not block the audience's view of the screen. Place the slide on the projector and then step well back. In practice, they tell you if you're in the way.

You need room beside the projector for two piles of slides – a 'before' and an 'after' pile – as well as your notes.

Give the audience time to read or copy the slide. Ask them if they would prefer you to read the slide out, or if they would prefer you to be quiet. Then elaborate on the points made on the slide.

If you want, you can mask parts of the slide using card or paper which can be moved down to reveal the next line or image. Sometimes it is worth the effort of attaching flaps with adhesive tape either to the transparency or a proper mounting frame. Similarly, a second slide can be affixed to produce an 'overlay'. This technique is particularly suited to the building up of complex diagrams or charts – each stage can be explained before the next element is introduced.

Using a flipchart   The flipchart is best used as a 'live' aid, for you to note down key words or sketch diagrams. Use big lettering that can be seen from the back of the room. Capital letters are usually more legible than script.

One problem with the flipchart is that it is difficult to keep neat lines of text. It may not matter, but if you think it does you can draw faint lines on the flipchart paper beforehand. It is also possible to buy lined or squared flipchart paper. Always have enough paper to last, and ensure that you have an adequate supply of the right kind of pen.

Using a whiteboard   Basically the same as for a flipchart, except that the pens must not be the permanent marker type. You will also need some means of cleaning the board – either a special board eraser, a cloth, or a paper hand towel.

Lesson

Many of the points about presentation techniques apply to the lesson as well. By lesson I mean an interactive training session. Typically, this will mean the trainer is giving some input and is using visual aids but is also interacting with the group. The group is no longer a passive audience but takes part in the session by making comments, questioning and giving its opinions. This is generally more enjoyable for them and, importantly, produces better understanding and learning. Preparation for a lesson is similar to preparation for a presentation but will include planning for interactive sections within the lesson. For example, an overhead projection slide about manpower planning might be followed by a question to the group: 'Who is responsible for manpower planning in your company?' The time to deal with the response must be estimated and allowed for. This can be quite difficult as, of course, you do not know what they are going to say. However, with experience you will be able to estimate more accurately. Also, you can adapt as you go along. If the session is behind schedule, you may make up time by simply telling them something rather than asking them to arrive at the answer for themselves.

In addition to presentation, the main techniques used in a lesson are as follows.

- Questioning and discussing
- Questioning and charting
- Asking for definitions
- Asking for examples from their experience
- Asking for reactions

Questioning and discussing

Trainer: Why do you think that people involved in car crashes often cannot remember the moment of impact?

Learner 1:   Because it's too frightening and so they blank it out.

Trainer: Possibly in some cases. But there's another reason

           relating to the model of memory we looked at yes-
           terday.

Learner 2: Is it to do with the information not having got
           from the short term memory store into the long
           term memory store before they've lost con-
           sciousness?

Trainer: Yes. Well done. Let me expand on that . . .

This approach stimulates people to think. It is very effective; but it has some pitfalls. You should never rubbish or put down a contribution. All contributions should be welcomed and rewarded. Try not to be patronizing when you do this though.

Trainer: Can anyone remember who developed the MUD
           taxonomy?

Learner: Was it Sylvia Downs?

Trainer: Oh well done Clive! You are clever. Isn't Clive clever
           everyone?

Also remember that people need to be told when they are wrong. Do it clearly, but in a way that makes them feel they are appreciated for having made an effort rather than have been told off for guessing wrongly.

Finally, know when to give up. If you keep asking and no one knows the answer, or they cannot understand the question, just tell them.

Questioning and charting Very useful when you know that the knowledge is present in the group. You can have a visual aid listing 'Uses for job descriptions', or you can instead ask:

Trainer: What uses are job descriptions put to in an organiz-
           ation? Call out and I'll write them on the whiteboard.

Learner 1: Job evaluation.

Trainer: Good. (*Writes 'Job evaluation' on board.*)

Learner 2: Recruitment.

Trainer: Yes, excellent. (*Writes 'Recruitment' on board.*)

Learner 3: Job grading.

Trainer: Wouldn't that come under job evaluation?

    Key points are:

• Write down exactly what they say unless they agree to your wording

- Don't reject points just because you didn't think of them
- Discuss points as they arise, or after they are all on the board, as you judge appropriate
- Make sure everyone gets a fair chance to join in

Asking for definitions   Often useful to stimulate thought: 'What do we mean by "motivation"? What is it?'
The key point is:

- Have a clear definition ready!

Asking for examples from their experience   'Has anyone here ever had to sack someone? You have, Jane. Would you be prepared to tell us about how you felt?' It is often better to get anecdotes from within the group rather than tell your own stories. It can be stimulating for you, and you learn from them as well as them learning from you.
Key points are:

- Have a fall-back story in case nothing comes out
- Be prepared to interrupt if someone starts a rambling and/or irrelevant story

Asking for reactions   'What do people feel about this model of learning? Is it useful?' A very good way to find out there and then what people's reactions are. It is valuable feedback for you. Do not become too defensive if they have opposite views to yours. It would be a strange world if we all agreed about everything.
Key points are:

- Listen carefully
- Be prepared to agree to differ

Room Layout

Training rooms can be arranged in a variety of ways. For a presentation, there are many possibilities that will

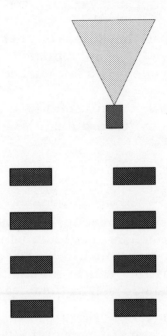

Example 4.4 Theatre-style room layout

work; for an interactive session, rather fewer. In a presentation, the main thing is that the presenter and his or her visual aids can be seen. For a group discussion, it is important that the learners can see each other. In some training situations, the trainer may wish to enter the middle of the group or walk around the edge of it. Options will be limited by the type of furniture available, the number of participants and the size and shape of the room. Some of the options available are discussed below.

Theatre style   In this arrangement the audience is seated in rows, as in a theatre (example 4.4). This enables the maximum number of people to be seated in a given area. Often hotels or other training venues will give a room capacity figure based on this layout, and this can be very misleading if you are not aware of what it means. Theatre-style layouts are fine for formal presentations but prevent

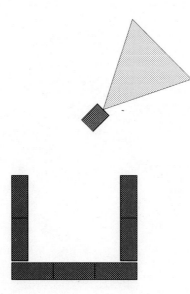

Example 4.5 Horseshoe room layout

members of the audience from interacting well with each other. Even making eye contact is difficult, except with the people seated next to each other.

Horseshoe The horseshoe, or U-shape, arrangement (example 4.5) is much more conducive to group inter-action. The trainer can also move into the middle of the group if desired. The main problem with this arrangement is that it limits the number of people that can be trained in a particular room.

Vee-shape A variation on the horseshoe (example 4.6). Some trainers feel that it facilitates eye contact better than the horseshoe. I use it if the tables are too big to arrange into a neat horseshoe.

Boardroom Boardrooms often double as training rooms. They tend to be dominated by huge tables (see example 4.7), and the learners sit around the circumference. This

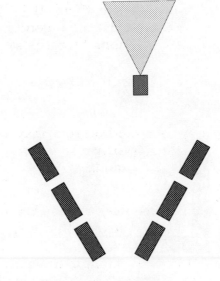

Example 4.6 Vee-shape room layout

Example 4.7 Boardroom layout

is not ideal as the trainer cannot enter into the middle of the group. Also, it limits options for the placing of visual aids so that everyone can see them. It is, however, an efficient use of space. It is also good when group members discuss issues among themselves.

Group Discussions

A group discussion is a method that may be used by a trainer to create a learning situation where attitudes and opinions are sought and examined. There are three key features of the process.

- The participative environment encourages the sharing of experiences and the introduction and development of ideas
- The fact that all the participants are actively involved in thinking, listening and speaking leads to better learning and fuller understanding
- Adults like to learn in this way

These effects do not, however, occur automatically. If the group knows little or nothing about a topic, then you are unlikely to get much of a discussion. Even if a topic is chosen that everyone knows something about, it may be difficult for the participants to get started if they are not given some help. Accordingly, before initiating a group discussion, the trainer has to prepare.

PRELIMINARIES

Not all topics are best taught by group discussion. Indeed the process itself may introduce no new facts to the group. What does happen, however, is the sharing of information held by the various group members (which may include the trainer). The process is valuable in the exchange of views and ideas, in problem solving and in the clarification of attitudes and understanding. You may, for example, choose to examine the ways in which a disciplinary situation might be handled by means of a group discussion. Because people will bring a range of different experiences with them, an interesting and lively discussion is likely from which group members will learn and attitudes may be altered.

Purposes The group discussion process may have various purposes.

- Disseminating knowledge about a subject
- Solving problems and making decisions
- Developing interpersonal skills
- Influencing attitudes
- Enlivening a training event
- Developing relationships within the group

Sometimes it is appropriate to have clearly defined learning objectives, sometimes not.

Environment People should be sitting fairly close to each other, ideally in a circle. If the group is too big, then some will not participate, so splitting into smaller groups may be appropriate. It may also be useful to provide flipcharts or other aids to assist the group. For some topics, privacy and confidentiality will be essential.

Getting started There are various ways in which the initial discussion may be stimulated. With some groups and some topics, it may work simply to say 'Now have a group discussion about topic X'. However, normally group discussions are more successful if they follow some other sort of input.

- Introductory talk or presentation
- Film or video
- Case study or written handout
- Exercise or game

For example, if you wanted to explore the topic of self-development you might try one of these approaches.

- A talk about the psychology of self-development
- A video about self-development
- A short case study highlighting self-development
- Asking who feels that they have contributed to their own career progression through self-development

How to achieve the objectives   Once you have got the discussion started, how will you make sure that your objectives will be achieved? What will you do if the participants are unable to see the points you had in mind? What if there is an adverse reaction to the topic, or someone gets upset?

The first time you try to create a group discussion of a topic, you will have little idea how long it will last and what degree of interest it will stimulate. It may also generate friction between the participants or lead to some participants being frozen out. As far as possible, you must prepare for all these eventualities. This may involve having back-up case study or presentation material, and you should think through how to handle any difficult situations which may arise.

CONTROL

The degree of control will vary according to the objectives of the trainer and the nature of the group. The skill of a trainer is in selecting the appropriate style of control as much as it is in exercising that control. The style may vary during the course of a discussion, with the trainer judging when it is right to intervene and when it is right to withdraw. The following three styles, therefore, may be considered as a range of options that merge into each other rather than as discrete entities.

Close control   The discussion leader controls the discussion by asking questions which are answered by group members directing the response to the leader. The leader may even decide who will contribute, and at which point, by naming who will respond, and may suppress uninvited contributions. Watch TV shows which involve audience discussion for examples of how this is done. The leader will evaluate all contributions and pass judgement in terms of 'That's right' or 'That's wrong'. The success of the discussion will be judged by him or her in terms of whether or not the group has reflected the leader's attitudes back to him or her.

This style is often employed where there is a specific problem to be discussed in a limited time. The degree of control, while high, is often not perceived as unwelcome by the group. Indeed, group participants may be impressed by the authority that is displayed. They feel they have participated but are aware of the high proportion of the leader's contribution, and may value this, particularly if they know they require such high control in order to be efficient.

The success of this style will depend to a large extent on the willingness of group members to accept it and the level of expertise of the leader compared that of the group. The style will lead to conflict or non-participation if the group resents the leader's approach. In particular, a group which been used to less control may react very negatively if this approach is adopted by a new course tutor.

Medium control   Here the trainer initiates the discussion but permits and encourages the group to talk to each other directly rather than through the chair. Some of the control mechanisms are suppressed, and the trainer leaves it to the group to evaluate contributions. He or she intervenes from time to time to expand on points that have arisen and to point the discussion in the required direction. This may be by encouraging certain individuals to expand their contributions, by stating 'Perhaps we are moving too far ahead', or by making some other such comment to restrict digression.

To encourage the group further to participate without going through him or her, the leader may sit among the group to reduce the emphasis on the leader role and may keep silent for quite long periods. If the discussion goes well, the leader does not interfere. This may sound easy, but not joining in a lively and interesting group discussion requires great restraint.

Low control The leader may withdraw from the discussion completely or may sit at the back of the room and observe, participating only when invited or when things are obviously going wrong. A group that is not used to this style often finds it uncomfortable to begin with. It tends to work better when the full group has been divided into smaller groups to discuss something. They then do not expect to be led.

The leader is invited to contribute facts or to give procedural advice. If the group asks for his or her opinion on the matter under discussion, he or she will avoid giving it. Instead, the leader will turn the question back to the group, or may state a number of different opinions to give the group something to work on.

The Facilitator Role

In the previous section the term 'leader' is used. However, it will be seen that in a medium-control or low-control situation, the trainer is actively avoiding leading the group for much of the time. The trainer may then be viewed as a facilitator who is there to help the group reach its objectives – and these may have been determined by the group, not the trainer.

In order for the trainer to function in a facilitating role, he or she must be perceived as a trustworthy person who understands what is happening and can be relied on to prevent conflict or personal antagonism getting out of hand. In particular, the facilitator may perform the following functions.

- Encouraging contributions, particularly from the less self-confident
- Ensuring the more verbose do not take over completely
- Controlling conflict by stepping in if necessary to divert the discussion to a less contentious issue, or by pointing out areas of agreement, or by analysing what has

caused the conflict so that the participants can take a more objective, less emotional, view

- Summarizing from time to time, and perhaps posing a question or making a suggestion to take the discussion forward
- Assisting quieter participants by rephrasing their arguments for them so that these do not get lost just because they are not forcefully put across. This may also be done by testing understanding of their contribution by questioning
- Ensuring individuals receive positive feedback from the group, perhaps by acknowledging contributions that the group ignores or by seeking positive contributions from others if a negative evaluation is given
- Providing feedback to the group as a whole as to its performance
- Providing the information and resources for the group to function effectively
- Staying quiet when all is well; permitting silences to allow time for people to think
- Ensuring that the discussion is brought to a close when the topic is exhausted
- Ensuring that the whole group attains common goals and derives its greatest satisfaction from having done this together

Running Exercises

Apart from devising your own exercises, it is nowadays possible to purchase collections of exercises or activities at very reasonable prices. These will often include instructions on how to use the material provided. However, you should always bear in mind that the people who wrote these instructions have probably been using the exercise in question for a few years. It is very easy for them to inadvertently leave out a key part of what they say or do, or for them to give you the impression that the exercise runs itself with no need for further input from you.

PREPARATION

The first thing you must do with any exercise that you are using for the first time is to read it thoroughly. You should be clear in your own mind what is likely to happen, and be satisfied that it will bring out the learning points which you require. Carefully study the list of resources needed and satisfy yourself that you have, or can get, everything necessary. If the instructions specify '30 metres of rope' how will you obtain this? I have certainly had bosses who would have taken a lot of persuasion to sanction such a purchase, whereas 'four rubber bands' seems perfectly manageable. Also read carefully what will be required in terms of the number of participants. Some exercises written for college classes require 20 or 30 people; others are designed for no more than 12. Some activities require an exact number of people, or require participants to work in threes (triads) or fours. Think what you would do with a group size of 11. Would it still work?

Assuming that you decide to proceed, clarify for yourself what preparation you will need to make. You may need a large space to work in, or syndicate rooms, as well as the materials specified. Remember to warn participants in advance if the exercise is likely to involve any physical exertion or the possibility of getting wet or dirty. Advise them so that they can dress appropriately. Otherwise, you may well find people reluctant to take part once they think that their clothes will be spoilt.

SAFETY

Be very careful with any activity that has a possibility of hurting people. For example, some activities ask the group to climb on to tables or to carry someone across a room. Unless you have a good reason for choosing such an exercise, try to find a safer substitute. Many years ago, when I was being trained as a trainer, our tutors organized a series of 'trust' exercises for us to experience. These included allowing oneself to fall backwards only to be saved by other members of the group. This worked well. Another activity was explained as follows:

> Everyone except George go and stand over by the wall. In a minute, we are going to ask George to close his eyes and run headlong at the wall. The rest of you will close around George with your bodies – cushioning him and preventing him from hitting the wall.

Unfortunately 'George' (I can't remember his real name) did not wait for the group to get ready, or for a signal from the trainers. Instead, he said 'Right', lowered his head and charged! The group scattered, leaving only me between George and the brick wall of the gym. I braced myself and thrust an elbow forward. George hit this at full pelt with the centre of his chest and then collapsed on the floor where he remained for several minutes looking very distressed. Eventually, he recovered. The exercise was abandoned, and I made a decision never to take part in, let alone run, such an exercise again. Presumably George did too. Most exercises do not have such dangers, and their use can greatly enliven a training course as well as facilitating experiential learning. There are some potential pitfalls though.

FACE VALIDITY

Sometimes the purpose of the activity may not seem obvious, and participants may demand it be explained before commencing. 'We work in insurance. How does this exercise about a car factory relate to us?' Face validity is a term used in psychometric testing to describe whether a test looks relevant – 'on the face of it' – to the characteristic it purports to measure. Tests with poor face validity are often not liked, even if they are very accurate. I think it is a useful term to use to assess the similar property in training activities. Be prepared to explain if asked, but also try to head off such objections by explaining before you are asked what the relevance of the exercise is. This is not always easy without giving too much away.

NON-PARTICIPATION

Some people may refuse to take part in some activities. This may be because they have a moral objection to the activity. For example, one popular exercise requires participants to pretend that they have to choose the order in which people will be rescued from a flooding cave. I have known people refuse to do this activity for ethical reasons, and this then leaves the trainer with a problem. Other people will not take part in any exercise that has military overtones.

Another reason why people refuse to participate is that they decide the activity is just too silly. There are exercises which ask people to communicate only by grunting, or to pretend to be farmyard animals. Know the group well before attempting such activities. Some people attend training events against their will and are looking for an excuse to refuse to participate in order to make a point. If you suspect this might happen and would prefer to avoid it, choose exercises with great care.

Many people will not take part happily in activities that require bodily contact with one another. An ice-breaking exercise I have in a book includes blindfolding people and asking them to mill around, getting to know each other 'by any means you choose, such as talking and touching'. This may be a perfectly valid activity, but it is one I would be very reluctant to try because I have met a lot of people who would refuse to do it.

However, this does not mean such activities should never be used. If you know the people concerned and believe that there is sufficient value in the activity to take the risk of objections or refusal, then go ahead. You can, of course, ask them whether or not they are prepared to try it. It is not normally a good idea to pressurize people to take part in an activity they have reservations about. Perhaps you can ask them to observe.

The section on dealing with difficulties (pages 133–41) considers other reasons for non-cooperation.

REVIEW

The purpose of an exercise, of course, is to stimulate learning. It is the trainer's job to ensure that the learning possibilities that lie within an exercise are fully exploited. This is done in the review process at the end of the activity. There are several ways to structure a review.

- Informal discussion
- Structured discussion
- Reports by observers
- Video playback
- Completion of a worksheet

Informal discussion   This is often the most popular way of reviewing an activity. Simply lead a discussion of what happened, making sure the key learning points are explored adequately.

Structured discussion   A discussion can be structured in that you can nominate who will speak and in what order. You can pose specific questions, perhaps writing them up, to direct the discussion.

Reports by observers   You may have asked one or more people to observe an activity. Their observations are fed back to the group before a discussion of what happened.

Video playback   The participants can watch themselves on video, and learning points can be drawn from the playback.

Completion of a worksheet   Participants may be asked to complete a worksheet, or 'review' sheet, which asks such questions as 'How well did your group work together?' This can either precede or follow a discussion.

Reading Group Dynamics

Before considering how to read group dynamics we must first define what we mean by the term 'group dynamics'. To do that, we must first define the term 'group'. Many definitions exist, but that by Brown (1988) is a suitable one for trainers:

> A group exists when two or more people define themselves as members of it and when its existence is recognized by at least one other.

The 'other' in this context may be other learners, managers or the trainer or trainers. If this definition is accepted, it follows that in one classroom of a dozen people it may be possible to find one group, or six groups or any other number in between. It is also possible to belong to more than one group at the same time, and therefore the potential number of groups can be much larger. For the sake of clarity, these groups-within-groups are often termed 'sub-groups'.

In practice, a group of 12 will often contain only two or three sub-groups that are identifiable to the trainer. Depending on the nature of the training you are conducting, it may or may not be important to make these identifications and to be aware of what is happening within each sub-group as well as the whole. In some kinds of training, such as team building, this awareness is absolutely central to the learning process.

The term 'group dynamics' describes the interactions and processes that occur within and between groups. These interactions include how relationships between individuals are formed and developed; the degree of group cohesion; how power is distributed and used; and how group norms are evolved and enforced. The processes include how the group is formed; how it resolves or tolerates conflicts; how it makes decisions; and how it copes with change.

It can be seen, therefore, that the study of group dynamics can be a highly involved and complex science.

There are some very heavy academic texts on the subject. However, some of the basic principles of how groups function can be readily understood. The reading of group dynamics is as much art as science, but a knowledge of the jargon used can make the description of group processes considerably easier. This can be of great assistance when trying to describe aspects of a group's functioning to others, or indeed to the group itself.

GROUP FORMATION

A descriptive system developed by Tuckman (1965) has entered the trainer's vocabulary largely because it is so easy to remember. This is the 'Forming, Storming, Norming and Performing' model, which you may be familiar with already.

The *forming* stage is when the group members do not yet know each other. There is some anxiety, testing out of the rules, and trying to find out what behaviour is acceptable. A trainer can reduce the anxiety felt by group members in various ways. For example, by organizing 'ice breaking' activities, or by discussing rules openly – 'it's okay to disagree', 'There will be no report back to your managers'. Some people feel anxious about what clothes to wear, and this anxiety can be reduced in the joining instructions so that everyone knows whether to wear either formal or casual clothes.

The *storming* stage may or may not happen. It is when conflict may surface between sub-groups and there may be a rebellion against the leader. The leader in a training context may be the trainer, and this stage can be quite uncomfortable. On a very short course there may not be enough time for the storming stage to evolve, and the individuals may consciously choose not to tackle issues that would otherwise concern them because they are aware that the group is a very temporary one.

The *norming* stage emerges after the storming stage has been resolved, the group can continue its development by establishing 'norms'. Norms are the tacitly agreed and understood ways of behaving which the group has evolved. They can include modes of dress, language, timekeeping, participation, etc. There is an open and healthy exchange of views and feelings.

The *performing* stage may never appear in some kinds of learning group. It is the stage when a team has emerged from the group and tasks are accomplished efficiently and effectively. Obviously, this stage may be required in a group of people who are going to be working together, but it is not relevant to people who will never see each other again. None the less, this stage can be reached in such circumstances, and some groups can feel a real sense of loss when a highly integrated group is disbanded at the end of a programme.

ANALYSING BEHAVIOURS IN GROUPS

It can often be interesting to observe a group performing a task or discussing something. It may be possible to assess what stage of development the group is at, the degree of cohesiveness it exhibits, and so on. It may also be useful to analyse communication patterns. This can be done for your own information, or can be fed back to the group for further discussion or analysis. The easiest kind of behaviour to analyse is verbal behaviour and several techniques are available to us to facilitate this.

Simple contribution analysis Record how many times someone speaks by simply making a tick or a mark against his or her name. As a rule of thumb, you may wish to define a contribution as any meaningful utterance of five words or more addressed to the group. You will then end up with a record of the contributions of the group members something like example 4.8.

How do we interpret this pattern? Perhaps it indicates that Clare and Louise are not participating fully. Perhaps it indicates that Jill does not know when to shut up. You will, of course, have heard the discussion as well as

Andy	√ √ √ √ √ √ √ √ √ √ √ √ √ √ √ √	16
Clare	√ √ √ √ √	5
Grahame	√ √ √ √ √ √ √ √ √ √ √ √ √	13
Jill	√ √	23
Mark	√ √ √ √ √ √ √ √ √ √	10
Louise	√ √ √ √	4

Example 4.8 Record of group members' contributions

simply scoring it, and so you will be in a better position to give feedback than simply from the numerical data.

Sequenced contribution analysis An alternative method is to record the person's contribution, perhaps by use of an initial letter, to show the pattern of the discussion. Using the names given above, we could end up with a pattern such as:

AJAJMAJLAJLAJAJAMCAJAJACAJACAJMLMAJACACAJA . . .

If we want to, we can still total up the number of contributions from each person. However, the pattern can tell us much more. If Andy has initiated the discussion, he is unwilling to let go of it. Also, after Andy has spoken, the next contribution has often come from Jill. Are they aware of this? Does it indicate favouritism or animosity? In fact, Jill has only ever spoken after Andy. Why is this?

Obviously, you will have much more information as you observed the discussion. This kind of evidence, though, when given as feedback to someone, can be much more powerful than your subjective impressions can be.

Directional contribution analysis Another way to record contributions people make is to represent them as circles on a piece of paper. If someone speaks, mark an arrow from the letter representing that person towards the

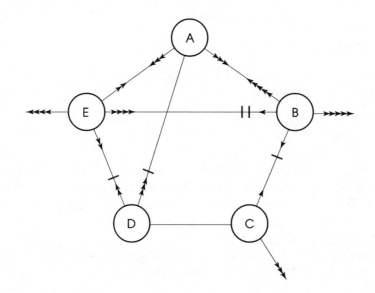

Example 4.9 Directional contribution analysis

To:	Alan	Betty	Charles	Diana	Total
From:					
Alan	–	8	6	14	28
Betty	7	–	3	11	21
Charles	14	2	–	1	17
Diana	9	7	1	–	17
Total	30	17	10	26	83

Example 4.10 Directional contribution analysis using a matrix

person they spoke to. Should the contribution be directed towards the group as a whole, then the arrow points outside the circle. (See example 4.9.)

An alternative method is to construct a matrix and use this to record the way contributions are made (example 4.10).

	Asks question	Offers answer	Positive contribution	Negative contribution
Alex				
Femi				
Mark				
Steve				
Ursula				

Example 4.11 Contribution analysis

Interaction process analysis   R. F. Bales (1950) invented a system for categorizing the contributions of group members in terms such as 'shows solidarity' or 'asks for opinion'. In all, Bales provided 12 categories for contributions to be assigned to. Since then, there have been a number of similar systems produced. The problem with Bales's system, and its derivatives, is that it is difficult for someone to assess where a contribution should go and record it before the next contribution has been made. I believe these more sophisticated systems have limited use for trainers. Perhaps they are manageable with the use of video recording, and the interested reader can find a fuller description of such systems in Rae (1995).

It is possible, however, to create your own more limited system to suit your specific needs (example 4.11). If you are feeding such information back to a group, then it is obviously going to be necessary to give examples of what you mean by 'positive' or 'negative' in this context; for example:

> We recorded 'I really don't like this kind of exercise' as a negative contribution, and 'I think we should go with Alex's idea' was recorded as a positive contribution.

OBSERVATION SHEETS

Apart from the detailed systematic approaches described above, it is also common to record what happened in more general terms. It is certainly not essential to have a prepared observation sheet, but many people find it helpful to have headings from which to work. As an alternative, it is possible to use a timed recording sheet. This gives some discipline to the recording process, which can be tedious, and ensures that observations are made at regular intervals. A sample of each type is given in examples 4.12 and 4.13, but it is often better to design your own to bring out the particular learning points that you want.

Dealing with Difficulties

First, it is not always possible to 'deal with' difficulties. Some difficulties will mean that the training event will fail to meet its objectives or must even be abandoned altogether. Second, one person's difficulty may be another person's attempt to get things put right. After all, if a learner believes that the training she is undertaking is inappropriate for her, we really should welcome the fact that she is going to say something about it even though this may be uncomfortable for us. However, we have to try to overcome difficulties that arise in order to achieve our objectives. When thinking about how the difficulty arose in the first place, always be prepared to examine your own conduct and be ready to learn from any mistakes you have made.

Unresponsive group

Some groups are more responsive than others. Sometimes the presence or absence of just one person makes a tremendous difference to the whole group. The reason the group is not responding must be ascertained before taking any action. Is the group always unresponsive? Or is it just with you? Is it this particular topic? Are they tired? The most unresponsive groups I have encountered were unresponsive because of poor identification of training needs or poor briefing by the line management.

Observation sheet

Use this sheet to record your observations. On the left-hand side of the sheet the time is given in minutes from commencement of the activity. On the right hand side, write down what is happening in the group every two minutes. Make notes about who is leading the activity, who is being left out or ignored, who is providing ideas, and so on. Do not take part at all, or voice any suggestions to the group. Your observations will be important in the discussion of how the group operated which will follow the activity.

Time started:

Minutes	Observations
0	
2	
4	
6	
8	
10	
12	
14	
16	
18	
20	
22	
24	
26	
28	
30	

Example 4.12 Chronological observation sheet

Observation sheet

Use this sheet to record your observations. Make notes under the headings given. Do not take part at all, or voice any suggestions to the group. Your observations will be important in the discussion of how the group operated which will follow the activity.

Time started:

The leader How did the leader organize the team? What did he or she do which was effective or ineffective?

Teamwork How did the group function together? Make notes about any particular behaviours which contributed to, or inhibited, success.

Decision making How were decisions made? Did the leader decide, or the group as a whole?

Record anything else of relevance or interest. Do not forget to note effective behaviour examples as well as ineffective behaviours.

Example 4.13 Leadership and teamwork observation sheet

However, we normally have to make do with the group we have, so select one or more of the following approaches to try to rectify the situation.

• Change the delivery style. Move from a lesson approach

to small-group work, with them reporting back. If the group is unresponsive because of laziness, make them work harder by requiring them to prepare a presentation.

- Give extra breaks.
- If the group has other things on its mind, allow time for these things to be got out of the way. I was once running a course for an organization whose staff union had just voted for industrial action. The group was preoccupied with this and was being unresponsive. One of them asked if they could have half an hour to discuss the implications of the vote. After that session, the group was back to its normal, responsive self.
- Break them up into small groups and ask them to come up with answers to the question 'How do we make this course livelier and more participative?' Be prepared for them to criticize you. Listen to any criticisms or suggestions and respond to them.
- Open the windows.
- Keep a score sheet to record who has contributed and who has not. Speak privately to those who have not participated and ask them why. If it is appropriate, tell learners that success on the programme is partly dependent on participation in the lessons and that their contribution rate is below the standard expected.
- If one or two people are deliberately not participating to make a protest, allow them to discuss it, but tell them that if they are not prepared to join in then they must leave. Be prepared to account for your actions afterwards. If throwing people out becomes a regular event, it may be you that is the problem.

HOSTILITY

If the group is hostile, it is probably because they do not recognize any value for them in the learning process that they are undertaking. This may be because of poor briefing, or it may be due to factors unconnected with the training itself. The group may be hostile to the concepts you are trying to purvey. For example, if you are trying to conduct a course on a new performance management system and the group believes the system will be used in a punitive fashion, then they will respond negatively to the training. On one occasion I started to deliver a course on appraisal to a group and was trying to sell the idea of appraisal as an indication of the management's concern for the long-term development of its employees. The group informed me that redundancies had been announced the day before and they were waiting to hear who was affected. Again, you have to try to assess the underlying reason for the problem as well as the likely outcome before selecting any of the following courses of action.

- Spend longer than you had planned explaining the reasons for the training and how it might benefit them.
- Ask them to tell you why they are angry. Listen carefully. Do not try to defend the indefensible, but acknowledge their feelings. Never say anything critical about the senior management that could be quoted to others out of context. After some of the heat has dissipated, ask them for agreement to carry on.
- Seek common ground. There is nearly always something you can agree with. If there are criticisms directed at you personally you can always say 'I'm sure I could do better'.
- If appropriate, agree to pass on complaints to whoever is concerned in return for the group's agreement to participate more fully in the course.
- Don't go on the attack. Stand your ground, but avoid criticizing the group. Remember, you are outnumbered!

CONFLICT

If there is conflict within the group, again you must try to understand why. Avoid exercises that promote conflict very early in a training course. Assess whether the conflict is a symptom of the group going through its storming stage. Is the conflict merely a resurfacing of old grievances?

- Control outright attacks by intervening. If someone is openly aggressive tell him or her that this is unacceptable behaviour. If necessary, remove the person concerned from the course.
- Allow other group members to contribute to the reconciliation process when appropriate.
- If two people have fallen out, keep them apart for a while when selecting syndicate groups. Put them together, perhaps a day or two later, to give them the opportunity to mend fences.
- Talk to the protagonists individually. Try not to take sides, but listen to both so that you can achieve an understanding of the reason for the conflict. Sometimes other group members will be able to explain to you what is going on.
- The conflict may be a symptom of a struggle for leadership or influence in the group. There may be little you can do other than contain it.

LEARNERS WHO ARE UPSET

Sometimes the learning process can be painful. Feedback, even if intended to be constructive and supportive, may in fact lead to people feeling attacked or hurt. Some of the people you may have on a training course can be extremely blunt and insensitive to one another. The fact that someone is upset may be indicated by a dramatic change in behaviour, such as crying, or by more subtle changes, such as withdrawing from the group. It is not always necessary or advisable to do anything. Many people get upset by a careless word, but are perfectly all right ten minutes later. However, sometimes action is needed. If someone has an emotional outburst and then runs out of the room, the trainer needs to take action. It is always a good idea to have at least two trainers involved in any training which is perceived as having a high risk of causing distress, such as training in bereavement counselling. One trainer can stay with the group while the other attempts to help the upset person.

- Allow someone who is upset some time and space to recover his or her composure. Protect them from any teasing or insensitive banter.
- Try to have a word with the person in private if you realize that something is wrong but do not know what. Adopt a counselling approach – that is, listening and empathizing – but recognize the person's right not to confide in you.
- Remember that someone can be upset because of domestic issues, or because of things happening in the workplace unconnected with training.
- It may be that one person's behaviour is upsetting someone else. Consider whether to have a quiet word with the person causing the distress.
- Someone who is upset because they are having trouble keeping up with the learning may need reassurance.
- Someone who is really upset is not going to learn anything. Let him or her leave the course to try to resolve the relevant issues.

SEXISM AND RACISM

One problem that may be encountered stems from the fact that some people express views which other people find offensive. Although there are many issues that can be involved, sexism and racism are two which are fairly frequently encountered. The trainer must ensure that no person is picked on or teased because of his or her gender or race. Apart from ethical considerations, failure to ensure equal opportunities within a course could lead to a complaint being made under the relevant legislation.

- Set a good example. Never tell racist or sexist jokes.
- If someone else tells such jokes, or makes other offensive remarks, you have a duty to stop him or her.
- Ensure that your handouts and visual aids are not racist or sexist. Videos should be selected with equal

opportunities in mind, although sometimes you may have to use what is available.

- Coarse language or vulgar behaviour by some course members may constitute sexual harassment towards others. If everyone thinks that the behaviour is acceptable and amusing – and if it is not disrupting the learning process – then it may be all right. But if just one person looks uncomfortable, embarrassed or distressed, that behaviour must be stopped or moderated.

TIMEKEEPING

Your carefully planned training can be ruined by poor timekeeping. Sometimes this is due to circumstances beyond the individual's control, but more often it is an attitudinal issue.

- Set a good example; ensure that you are always in the room early.
- Start promptly, even if some people have yet to arrive.
- If it is not appropriate to start before some people have arrived, consider asking the group that is there to discuss 'How should we handle the problem of people arriving late?' Ask latecomers to join the group and contribute.
- Arrange for coffee to be available up to the proper starting time. Have it removed then so that latecomers have to wait for coffee until the first break.
- Is the starting time reasonable? Discuss it with the group and agree a definite time that they all commit to arrive by.
- Ask people who arrive late to stay behind so that you can tell them what they have missed.

DOMESTIC ARRANGEMENTS

Many courses are ruined by problems associated with the domestic arrangements. Although these are problems that really should not affect the learning process, the fact is that they do. It is not possible to foresee every contingency, but some problems can be avoided by careful planning.

- Check with the person responsible for safety in your organization that your training venue is suitable, and ensure that you comply with any legal requirements.
- Ensure tea and coffee are available. Check if anyone requires decaffeinated products.
- Check if anyone has special dietary needs. Offer a vegetarian alternative if lunch is provided.
- Cater for smokers.
- Inform people of car-parking arrangements, where the nearest station is, etc.
- Know where the nearest telephone, toilet, first-aid point and fire exits are.
- You may need to ban mobile telephones, bleepers or other interruptions.
- Check accessibility for any learners with mobility problems.

Summary

This chapter has dealt with a number of different delivery methods, and has also looked at some of the things that go on within groups in the training context. Aspects of delivery which have been discussed include:

- presentations
- lessons
- group discussions
- running exercises
- group dynamics
- dealing with difficulties

Trainers must experiment with techniques, and evolve their own style and range of methodologies. Training delivery is, of course, an interactive process. What works well with one group may fall flat the next time. It is not possible to get it right every time, but trainers who are consistently well received have five things in common. They:

- prepare thoroughly
- respect and care about the learners
- are flexible and responsive
- let their personalities come out through the training
- enjoy training

ACTIVITIES

1 Presenting a case to gain commitment

Introduction Apart from the basic skills of presentation, trainers need to learn to be effective as persuaders. This is an activity which requires the presenters to structure a case so as to convince others to support it.

Aims To provoke thought and discussion about how a case should be structured in a training context, and to provide an opportunity to present and defend a training proposal.

Method Divide the group into teams of three or four. Each team is asked to prepare a presentation about one of the following.

- Purchasing some new training equipment
- Refurbishing training facilities
- Recruiting an additional trainer
- Recruiting an additional/new training administrator
- Spending a large sum of money on a management development programme
- Increasing the length of an existing training programme

Each team then takes turns to make its presentation to the rest of the group. When being presented to, the group role-plays senior managers and asks probing questions to which the presenters must respond. Each presentation is then assessed by the group. Discussion is focused on the factors which made one presentation more persuasive than another. The assessment sheet shown in example 4.14 may be useful for this activity.

Timing Allow an hour for preparation, ten minutes per team for presentation and around 20 minutes for discussion.

2 Leading group discussion

Introduction Rather than simply practising discussion leading with an irrelevant topic, this activity produces both skill practice for the person leading the discussion and learning through discussion for the rest of the group.

Aims To provide skill practice in leading group discussion and learning about training-related subjects.

Method Following input and discussion about leading group discussion, each learner selects a topic. Each must choose a different topic. They then prepare to introduce the topic and conduct a group discussion on it. For a large group, people may work in pairs. You could select topics from the following.

- Outdoor training and development
- Training venues
- Distance learning
- Role play
- Interesting ways to start training courses
- Equal opportunities in training
- New technologies in training
- Should training and personnel be separate?

Feedback is then given, together with discussion about points of technique. The assessment sheet shown in example 4.15 may be useful for this activity.

Introduction		Comments
Introduced self/team	☐	
Introduced subject	☐	
Stated the range of the presentation	☐	
Making a case		
Explained the need for the change/the problem to be solved	☐	
Demonstrated that alternative solutions had been considered	☐	
Put forward persuasive arguments	☐	
Presentation		
Structure	☐	
Pace	☐	
Clarity	☐	
Answering questions	☐	
Use of visual aids	☐	
Effectiveness	☐	
Timing	☐	
Comments:		

Example 4.14 Assessment – presentation of a case

Introduction		Comments
Introduced self	☐	
Introduced subject	☐	
Explained the need	☐	
Stated the objective of the session	☐	
Control		
Involvement of all participants	☐	
Keeping to subject	☐	
Dealing with aggression and/or disruption	☐	
Answering questions	☐	
Summarizing	☐	
Effectiveness of discussion	☐	
Timing	☐	
Comments:		

Example 4.15 Assessment – group discussion leading

Timing Although extensive preparation is not necessary, most people like to think about the topic for some time before the activity. Therefore, perhaps allow people to prepare overnight. The discussions may be limited to, say, 20 or 30 minutes as required. Feedback and discussion of the process takes a further ten minutes per discussion.

3 Group dynamics exercise

Introduction   A short exercise that is quite memorable.

Aims   To clarify understanding about the effect of goal clarity on group functioning.

Method   One or two people are asked to observe the rest of the group undertaking two short group exercises. Any method of recording or observation may be used.

1 Tell the group that you will give them a question to discuss about group dynamics, and that they will not be allowed to ask any questions. Then show the group the following question, prepared on the flipchart or overhead slide in advance:

   What are the most significant considerations regarding group dynamics to be borne in mind when facilitating intergroup interactions using analogous communication as opposed to multilateral logical syntax?

2 Show the group the following question, prepared on the flipchart or overhead slide in advance:

   What examples can you give of team activities which a teenager might take part in?

The exercise is concluded by feedback from the observers and discussion about the effect of goal clarity on group dynamics, relating this to training situations.

Timing   Allow five minutes for each question, followed by about 15 minutes discussion.

FURTHER READING

Bales, R. F. 1950: *Interaction Process Analysis: A Method for the Study of Small Groups*. Chicago: University of Chicago Press.

Brown, R. 1988: *Group Processes: Dynamics Within and Between Groups*. Oxford: Basil Blackwell.

Kolb, D. A., Rubin, I. M. and Osland, J. S. 1995: *Organizational Behavior: An Experiential Approach* (6th edn). Englewood Cliffs: Prentice-Hall.

Rae, L. 1995: *Techniques of Training* (3rd edn). Aldershot: Gower.

Schindler-Rainman, E. 1988: *Taking Your Meetings Out of the Doldrums* (revised edn). San Diego: University Associates.

Stuart, C. 1988: *Effective Speaking*. London: Pan.

Tuckman B. W. 1965: Development sequences in small groups. *Psychological Bulletin*, 63, 384–99.

5

Assessment and Evaluation

There is nothing so useless as doing efficiently that which should not be done at all.
Peter F. Drucker, Chambers Book of Quotations

Overview

There has probably never been as much emphasis on the assessment of performance and the evaluation of training as there is now. Assessment impacts on training in various ways. First, there is assessment to identify learning needs. Second, there is assessment in order to certify competence, often linked to qualifications but also linked to performance management. Third, there is assessment as part of the selection process in recruitment and also in development. Fourth, there is assessment in order to prove the effectiveness or otherwise of the training process. This is the area where assessment forms part of the evaluation process.

Evaluation of training has a far higher profile now than it did in the past. As a profession, training has long promised 'Give us the resources and we'll transform the business'. Line management is now replying 'Prove it'. There is a requirement to prove the connection between an investment in training and an improvement in organizational performance. While this is understandable, it creates some difficulties for trainers. The fact is that the benefits of sustained, long-term, investment in training are usually impossible to calculate accurately. An organization that has sanctioned a major increase in training expenditure will also be doing other things differently. There will be new managers, new products, new markets, and so on. However, it is not acceptable to use this as a rationale to justify lack of accountability, and trainers must be able to make some estimation of the impact of their efforts or lose credibility.

Assessment and evaluation in training have also been emphasized through government initiatives, in the United Kingdom at least. The National Vocational Qualification (NVQ) system has assessment at its very heart. Indeed, it has created a whole army of people who do nothing else but assess, as well as a legion of others who check these assessments. The Investors in People award requires organizations to perform assessments in various areas. In particular, for an organization to become an 'Investor in People', it must evaluate the investment in training and development to assess achievement and improve future effectiveness. Organizations seeking the award are required to evaluate training at individual, team and organizational levels. The NVQ system helps organizations to do this, although it is not the only way to do so.

Unfortunately, the undoubted benefits to be gained from rigorous assessment and evaluation are offset, to some degree at least, by some of the downsides. Really thorough assessment and evaluation processes are time consuming, bureaucratic and expensive. The line manager likes the idea that the training function must prove its worth. What he or she does not always like is the involvement he or she must give to this process. In many instances, assessments must be carried out by the line management in the workplace. Some assessment systems are perceived as being complex and bureaucratic, and this can result in alienation.

Similarly, any meaningful assessment system has to include assessing some people as falling below the standard required. This can bring a schoolroom atmosphere to training which can have a negative impact on the learning process. At the time of writing, the NVQ system in the United Kingdom has attracted strong support in some organizations but little or none in many others. If an organization embraces NVQs wholeheartedly, then the system produces a framework for assessment which provides a process both for the identification of training needs and for the evaluation of learning. It also provides a comprehensive record system. All this costs money and, unless it is funded adequately, the introduction of NVQs can result in less training activity rather than more. UK trainers interested in the NVQ system should contact the National Council for Vocational Qualifications (see Appendix 1). Alternatively, make contact with your local Training and Enterprise Council (TEC). In Scotland, the equivalents are Scottish Vocational Qualifications and Local Enterprise Companies (LECs).

Trainers interested in the Investors in People award can also contact the local TEC or LEC, or Investors in People UK, Investors in People (Scotland), or The Training and Employment Agency in Northern Ireland (see Appendix 1 for details).

Some aspects of assessment are dealt with in chapter 1 which deals with the identification of training needs.

Evaluation

It is generally accepted that there is a strong case for attempting to evaluate training, particularly in view of the very large sums of money which are spent on it. However, there are a number of problems associated with the evaluation process which must be considered.

The first difficulty is that, in an ideal world, it would be necessary to measure the exact knowledge and skill of each trainee before the start of the training. Without this information it is impossible to assess what has been learned by the end. What someone is capable of doing at the end of the training may primarily reflect what they could do before the training. To separate out the new learning may necessitate a pre-test, which is practicable in some learning situations but becomes much more difficult in other situations. For example, if we were to introduce the pre-testing of senior managers before a course on leadership, then we could anticipate some resentment which could actually inhibit learning. With subjects such as assertiveness, someone's ability to display assertive behaviour could be greatly reduced by the anxiety generated by the assessment process. Pre-testing in many situations may also inhibit the process of establishing rapport with the course members, and can result in the learning experience becoming a 'what do I have to do to get through it' ordeal. Sensitivity must be applied to any assessment process.

Another difficulty is that an ongoing review tends to result in changes to the detail of the programme before it can be thoroughly evaluated. It is not sensible to say to line managers, 'I know it's not working, but I want to prove that systematically before changing it'. Sometimes a rigorous evaluation methodology must be sacrificed for the sake of expediency.

A third difficulty is the sheer workload that thorough evaluation can require. Although evaluation is important, is it more important than delivery or design? What would the senior management rather you spent your time on? Many line managers can be convinced of the importance of evaluation, but most would not want to see it taking up more than a small proportion of the trainer's time. They would rather see you training than evaluating. Before approaching an evaluation project, we must ask ourselves the following questions.

WHY IS THE EVALUATION REQUIRED?

There are various reasons for evaluating training. Evaluation:

- enables the effectiveness of an investment in training to be appraised which can help to justify expenditure on future programmes
- allows the effectiveness of differing approaches to be compared

- provides feedback to the trainers about their performance and methods
- enables improvements to be made, either on the next occasion or, if the evaluation is ongoing, as the training proceeds
- can be motivational for learners
- indicates to what extent the objectives have been met and therefore whether any further training needs remain

WHAT SHOULD BE EVALUATED AND WHEN?

A number of different models have been developed by various writers. The structure below is that put forward by Kirkpatrick (1976). It is one of the most widely used frameworks and is relatively straightforward. An alternative system devised by Warr Bird and Rackham (1970) is discussed by Sanderson (in Truelove, 1995); and that by Whitelaw (1972) and Hamblin (1974) is discussed by Reid Barrington and Kenny (1992).

KIRKPATRICK'S LEVELS OF EVALUATION

Level 1 – Reaction The participants' opinion of the materials, facilities, methods, content, trainers, duration and relevance of the programme. What did the learners think about the training?

Level 2 – Learning The skills, knowledge and attitudes learned during the programme. Have the learning objectives been met?

Level 3 – Behaviour The change in on-the-job performance which can be attributed to the programme. Did the learning transfer to the job?

Level 4 – Results The effect on the organization of the changes in behaviour, such as cost savings, quality improvements, increases in output. Has the training helped departmental or organizational performance?

These are sequential stages in the process. If the link between training and *results* is to be established, then the effect of the training on *behaviour* must be demonstrated by proving that the *learning* was a result of the training. If the learners do not endorse this relationship in their *reactions* then the effectiveness of the training will not be believed.

WHAT KIND OF MEASUREMENT WILL BE USED?

Different approaches are appropriate for each level of evaluation.

Level 1 Questionnaires, interviews, group discussion or asking trainees to write a report can be used. Care must be taken with all these methods. Very often participants have enjoyed a course, even if they learned very little. Factors such as the quality of the lunch provided, or the comfort of the chairs, may influence the assessment of the training given. The other participants may have spoilt a basically sound course, or conversely saved a basically poor course.

Trainees are not always in a position to know immediately whether what they have learned will be useful and it may be best to wait some considerable time before asking for an opinion. Sometimes a trainee may have felt unfairly criticized during a course, and so may rubbish it in retaliation. I also feel that the more training a person receives, the more critical they are likely to become. Their standards and expectations rise with experience.

Using more than one technique can be helpful to gain a broader picture. Also look out for cues such as an increase or decrease in demand for the training (where there is choice), or if the line managers start asking for one particular trainer in preference to another.

Level 2 Tests, examinations, workplace based assessments of competence, projects or attitude questionnaires are the key techniques here. Some learning situations are easy to test for (e.g. typing ability), whereas others necessarily involve a good deal of subjectivity (e.g. counselling skills). Yet other learning is so long term in its nature that direct methods are frankly not appropriate. For example, if a newly appointed supervisor attends a course then an end test or examination can only tell us if he or she has learned certain terms, concepts or models. It cannot tell us if he or she will become a good supervisor by applying that learning in the work situation.

The processes used at level 2 are often termed 'validation'. This term is considered later on in this section.

Level 3 Requires assessment of improved performance on the job. This is easiest in jobs where before and after measures can easily be made (e.g. the speed at which an insurance proposal form can be processed). It becomes more difficult to evaluate performance in jobs which are less prescribed and measurement is imprecise (e.g. training design). There may be a time-lag between training and the appearance of indicators of performance improvement. For instance, returning to work after attending a course on leadership, a manager may immediately practise what she has learned – but the results of this take two or three months to become apparent. During that time other factors in the situation may have changed – there may have been some new staff recruited, or some redundancies may have affected morale. If we were to instigate a long-term assessment process, we would also find it difficult to separate out the influence of day-to-day experience from the influence of the formal training course. It is often impossible to isolate the precise influence of the training. Often the trainer has to resort to indirect performance assessment measures to gauge the influence of the training.

Level 4 Because departmental and organizational results depend on many people and it is difficult to attribute improvements to the efforts of specific individuals, evaluation at this level often has to be conducted in a more general way. Does the overall training programme result in greater efficiency, profitability or whatever? If we were to try to look at the impact of a large training programme on a part of a large organization, then we can take an experimental approach. Ideally, we take two identical units. One is given lots of training, the other is given none. Two years later, the difference in performance is apparent.

Obviously such an approach is not one which can be easily advocated. If we really believe that the training is likely to be of value, it is unfair, perhaps even unethical, to withhold it from one of the units in order to conduct an experiment. However, it is sometimes possible to obtain historical information which shows a correlation between spending (or some other measure) on training and organizational performance. Perhaps two similar units within the same organization can be compared and the relationship between past training activity and other measures can be assessed (e.g. accident rate, machine downtime, customer complaints).

COST–BENEFIT ANALYSIS

One of the key ways in which level 4 evaluation can be tackled is to attempt to calculate the benefit of the training in relation to the cost of the training. Cost–benefit analysis is a way of determining whether a particular solution has produced a greater financial benefit than the cost incurred. As an approach, it can also be used in advance to assess whether a particular training solution is likely to make sense financially. It may be a fundamental requirement of senior managers asked to approve a costly solution.

Steps

1 Determine the time period to which your analysis will apply.
2 Generate a list of cost factors related to the solution.
3 Determine the cost associated with each factor (roughly for an initial analysis; accurately at later stages in a proposal or for evaluation).
4 Total these costs.
5 Determine the financial benefits of the solution.
6 Express the results as a ratio: $\dfrac{\text{Benefits}}{\text{Costs}}$.

Example Let us consider sending two members of staff on a training course.

Cost of training two existing tele-sales staff by sending them on a three-day course:

Course fees	£450 × 2	= £900
Travel	£90 × 2	= £180
Hotel	£160 × 2	= £320
Coverage by agency temps while away	£300 × 2	= £600
Total		**£2,000**

It is hoped that the training will improve sales performance by ten per cent. The estimated value of these increased sales is therefore 10 per cent of the current annual sales of £300,000; that is, £30,000 p.a. per person.

The profit margin is 20 per cent, so the value of the benefit is £6,000 (20 per cent of £30,000) per person. For both of them the benefit would be £12,000 p.a.

We might need to know how long this benefit would last. The personnel department tells us that tele-sales staff stay, on average, 18 months. Therefore, the benefit = £12,000 × 1.5 = £18,000.

The cost–benefit calculation is:

$$\frac{\text{Benefits}}{\text{Costs}} = \frac{£18,000}{£2,000} = £9, \text{ i.e. for every £1 spent £9 is made}$$

At the proposal stage, this should be amply persuasive. However, the manager of the sales department should also want to ensure that these projected sales actually happen. Therefore, the calculation must be performed again after a suitable period to check whether the antici-pated benefits have actually come through. Suppose that they have. The sales manager, now very enthusiastic about training and evaluation, has six new members of staff. Why not send each of them to a different training provider, and calculate the cost–benefit ratio in each case? The only pitfall here is that the results may reflect the natural talent of the individual concerned rather than the skill of the training provider. However, as an approach it is basically sound and can be used in many types of evaluation to compare different options.

The increased sales scenario is comparatively easy to measure. In other situation more complex measurements must be attempted. Costing can be a very complicated exercise indeed, but a simple approach is often enough to enable judgements to be made in the training situation. Firstly, let us consider how to cost training in two types of training situation.

- On-the-job training
- Off-the-job training

On-the-job training is the term applied to learning while working within the normal work area and actually doing the job. Thus, a trainee gardener who is pruning roses in a public park and who is under guidance from an experi-enced gardener is receiving on-the-job training. Similarly, trainee shop assistants dealing with real customers or trainee machinists making 'real' products are receiving on-the-job training.

Off-the-job training is the term applied to classroom training, or to training outside working hours using machinery that is not 'live'. Instead of real customers, perhaps the trainees are taking it in turns to role-play customers.

The key costs in on-the-job training are:

- trainees' wages and other employment costs
- loss of production/sales/etc.
- any additional payment made to the instructor
- value of any excess materials used
- value of any excess damage or spoilage

The key costs in off-the-job training are:

- trainees' wages and other employment costs
- trainers' wages and other employment costs
- value of the materials used
- depreciation of equipment
- overheads

Suppose we look at a fictitious example of how these costings can be used as an evaluation measure. Let us assume that it currently takes 20 weeks for someone to learn how to perform a production job. The trainee costs the company £150 a week to employ. During the 20 weeks the trainee is an additional person to the regular operator, and so all the employment costs must be included. The operator is paid an instructor's allowance of £5 per week for the period. At the beginning, the output is much reduced as the operator has to explain everything slowly, and the machine speed is purposely reduced. Also, more of the raw materials are spoiled than would normally be the case. Fortunately (as in real life), we can get the value of these items from the management accountant. The costs look like this:

The trainees' wages and other employment costs	£150 × 20 = £3,000
The loss of production	£4,000
The additional payment made to the instructor	£5 × 20 = £100

The value of any excess materials used	£900
Total	**£8,000**

The training department then restructures the training to make it off-the-job. It decides to take in six trainees at a time. Because the training is full time, the trainees become fully proficient in only ten weeks. The trainer's salary and employment costs for those ten weeks amounts to £5,000. Materials consumed amount to £1,500. The machinery used depreciates by £2,500, and the overheads amount to £6,000 – mainly due to the cost of the room being used. The sums now look like this:

The trainees' wages and other employment costs	£150 × 10 × 6 = £9,000
The trainer's wages and other employment costs	£5,000
The value of the materials used	£1,500
Depreciation of equipment	£2,500
Overheads	£6,000
Total	**£24,000**

However, this is the cost of training six people so the cost per head is only £4,000 compared with the on-the-job system cost of £8,000 per head. Obviously, this is a simplified example. In many instances the various cost elements can be difficult to quantify, but usually a reasonable estimate can be obtained. Also note how many of the costs of off-the-job training continue when no training is being performed. If the training facilities are used only once a year, then the sums should really include the depreciation and overheads for the full year when calculating the costs.

This approach can be used in many situations to measure whether changes to the training arrangements are paying off, and therefore whether to continue with them or seek out more cost-effective solutions. An extended discussion of costing can be found in Harrison (1992).

VALIDATION

There are differences of opinion as to what this term actually means. I stated before that the processes at level 2 in Kirkpatrick's system were sometimes termed validation. This usage is supported by many writers. For example, Anderson (1993) states:

> the emphasis on evaluation is on value; the emphasis on validation is meeting specific objectives.

Evaluation is sometimes defined as being different and separate from validation. In my view, validation is a form of evaluation. It is concerned with answering the question 'Did the training meet its objectives?' (level 2). This is not the same question as 'Was this training worthwhile in business terms?' (level 4), or 'Are people using this learning on the job?' (level 3). To complicate matters further, some trainers use the term to describe reaction evaluation (level 1). For example, Rae (1995) talks at length about 'end-of-course validation questionnaires'. Others use the term to consider whether the objectives of the training were the right ones (therefore valid) in the first place. The term is also used by many people as a synonym for accreditation by an external body.

It is not actually necessary to use the term at all, and if it causes confusion, perhaps it is best avoided.

REACTION EVALUATION

There are several reasons why we may want to record the reaction of learners to a training event. This is an easy and quick way to achieve some form of evaluation and, although of limited scope, it often gives useful information. Reaction evaluation forms are used to:

- assess the level of satisfaction with the course

- enable learners to express their views and feelings about the learning
- give feedback to the trainer so that improvements may be made to the training
- give a quality control mechanism
- link the training to the workplace
- assess domestic and resource provision, and possibly compile evidence for improvements to facilities

There are many different ways to construct reaction evaluation forms and many ways to use them. When designing a form, try to think through what information you really want to know. It is possible to design a form in a manipulative way, asking people to praise you rather than say what they really think, but there is little point to this. I once co-tutored a course in a company which used a form which had several levels of satisfaction available. If the learners ticked the highest category, that was all they had to do and could leave. If they ticked any other category, they had to explain why. We got very good marks!

When considering what questions to include in the form, remember that there is often no benefit to the individual who is actually completing the form. For him or her, the training is over. It has come and gone; and whatever changes are made are of only academic interest to the person concerned. If the form is to be completed at the end of the course, perhaps a few minutes before 'home time', the learners will not want to spend a long time filling in an elaborate form and providing in-depth analysis. Therefore, in my view, we should make the form quick and simple to complete, whilst at the same time allowing the learners an opportunity to express their views.

Sometimes organizations prefer to allow people time to consider their views before completing a reaction evaluation form. A disadvantage of this is that many people forget to complete the form. If they have to be chased, then they are not likely to give the form much

Training evaluation form

Please take a few minutes to complete this form and return it to the tutor on completion of your course. Your feedback is important to us, and will be taken into account when running future courses. If you need more room for your comments, please use the back of the form.

Thank you,

Steve Truelove

Course title:................................. Tutor(s):...

Held at:.. From: .... To: ....

Your name: ....

Job title:.. Company:...

Assessment		Comments
Did you identify your learning objectives before attending the course?	☐Yes ☐No	
Did you discuss these with your manager?	☐Yes ☐No	
To what extent were your objectives met?	☐Fully ☐Substantially ☐To a small extent ☐Not at all	
Do you think the design of the course or the material in it should be changed?	☐Yes – substantially ☐Yes – slightly ☐Don't know ☐No	
How competent was the trainer at delivering this course?	☐Very good ☐Good ☐Satisfactory ☐Below the standard expected	
What is your overall rating of the course?	☐Very good ☐Good ☐Satisfactory ☐Below the standard expected	
Anything you would like to add?		

More comments on the other side of this form ☐

Example 5.1 Reaction evaluation form

Performance	Conditions	Standards
Mow the lawn	An electric mower in good condition	No areas missed
	Square or rectangular flat lawn	No cuttings left
	Initial grass length 3–5 cm	Clear straight line pattern
		No scalping
	Dry grass	At the rate of 600 square metres per hour

Example 5.2 Objective

consideration anyway. A sample form is given in example 5.1. For fuller discussion of reaction form design, the book by Rae (1995) is recommended.

Assessment Methods

There are a range of methods available to trainers for assessment. Which one to use will depend on a number of factors, in particular, the type of learning involved – memory, understanding or doing – and the situation in which it is to be applied. It is best to be as direct as possible in assessment, but there are times when indirect methods are needed.

CRITERION-REFERENCED ASSESSMENT

This is a term used to describe an assessment against a clear objective standard. In performance terms, it relates directly to behavioural objectives. Can the person do something under specified circumstances to a specified standard or not? In chapter 2 we looked at the way behavioural objectives were written. Example 5.2 shows again the example we gave in that chapter (example 2.1).

It should now be blindingly obvious how to assess whether learning has been achieved which meet these objectives. We need to get the learner to demonstrate his or her performance, under these conditions, and we need to have an assessor who will be rigorous and consistent in determining whether the criteria for the performance – the standards – have been met.

Even in the straightforward example given, there is the potential for variation. Would one blade of grass left on the lawn disqualify the person? Do we need to measure straightness with a theodolite or will doing so by eye be good enough? The problem gets worse with objectives, however well defined, which contain inherently subjective elements or which are hard to observe or quantify. This can lead to an emphasis on the assessment of what is easy to assess rather than what is important. For example, someone delivering a presentation is easy to assess in terms of time management and usage of visual aids. He or she is much harder to assess in terms of effectiveness. This does not mean that we should not try to make such assessments, but that we must strive to make such assessments as consistent and meaningful as possible.

For the assessment of observable performance skills – such as lawn mowing, shirt making, typing and bricklaying – criterion-referenced assessments should always be used. For performance concerned with conceptual or interpersonal skills, criterion-referenced assessment is less meaningful, and other methods have to be employed in order to make a judgement about competence. In the NVQ system, the forms of evidence considered can include written documentation, written reports probed by questioning and witness testimony. One of the criticisms of assessments of this nature is that they are awarded as much for skill in presenting evidence as for true competence.

ESSAYS

In the context of assessment, an essay is an answer to a question in the form of continuous writing in which the writer has considerable discretion in terms of how to express himself or herself. Essays can be of indeterminate length or may be subject to some sort of limit (e.g. between two and four pages). Essays can be set as part of a continuous assessment programme or as part of an examination. There are three purposes for the use of an essay as an assessment device – to assess:

• the command of language and the ability to express oneself in writing
• the level of knowledge and understanding of a particular subject matter
• the ability to interpret facts and to analyse the relationship between them

The first of these purposes is probably of more concern in educational contexts than in training, although it can be useful in selecting people for employment or promotion if such abilities are required. The second purpose is often seen as part of the learning process as well as assessment. If the learner is required to read up certain information in order to write the essay, then that can improve both memorization of the facts and understanding of them. Lack of understanding is often readily apparent in an essay. The third purpose is often of great relevance in a training situation. It is a way of assessing if the information given in the classroom (or wherever) can be used to understand a particular situation.

In an examination, the examiner may set a question as 'open book', which means that the learners can bring books and/or notes in with them. This has the advantage of reducing the pressure to memorize information prior to the examination, and allows the learner to concentrate more on interpretation and analysis. Obviously, an open-book examination is not an appropriate means of assessing the retention of factual information. One problem with open-book examinations, and also in essays set as course work, is that some people simply copy out a section of a book or handout material to answer a question. Care must be taken in the setting of the question, and in the instructions to the learners, to ensure that the abilities under study are going to be displayed.

Marking of essays is always subjective to some degree. In order to allow the writer discretion with regard to essay content, it does not make sense to have a very rigid marking scheme. However, if the essay is primarily designed to test retained knowledge, it is possible to put in a structure which gives points for the inclusion of specific facts (e.g. the names of key competitors). In most situations where essays are appropriate, marking will have to be a mixture of looking at the content and the interpretation. It is good practice to let people know the marking balance in advance so that they can apportion their efforts appropriately. For example:

> Outline a model of team roles that you are familiar with (40 per cent of marks) and describe how such a model can be used in the selection and training of personnel for a project team (60 per cent of marks).

If you are marking a number of essays, it is helpful to read rapidly through all of them to gain a general idea of the standard. Initially, make no notes or marks. Then read through more carefully, perhaps sorting the essays out into piles of 'good', 'average', and 'poor'. Each pile can now be re-examined carefully, and the relative merits of each essay considered. Marking essays is essentially a comparative process. When you start, you have little idea of what you would regard as good or poor, but a picture will gradually emerge. The number of piles you end up with may depend on the number of grades or marks you will give. A three-point scheme of 'fail', 'pass' and 'merit' might be adequate. At the other extreme there are percentages – with a theoretical range of zero to 100. In practice, percentages are usually given to the nearest five points and the range is more likely to extend from about 40 to 80 or 90. This gives a range of seven or nine increments.

Sometimes learners will say, 'I only got 60 per cent.

Where did I lose the other 40 per cent?' To reduce misunderstandings, try to give guidance beforehand about how you mark. For example, say: 'The top mark I have ever given for this topic was 95 per cent. This was a quite exceptional essay which brought in ideas which we hadn't covered in the course, and involved a lot of library research. A mark of around 80 per cent would be very high, and on average only about one in ten people score at that level. A good mark would be around 60 to 70 per cent. The pass mark is 50 per cent. If you score below this level, I will talk to you about how to improve your marks and let you try again.'

Even then, you will have to explain, and if necessary defend, the marks you have given. Usually, the essay will have a learning purpose as well as an assessment purpose, and the process should, as far as possible, remain a motivating one for the learners.

PROJECTS

Many of the points about essays also apply to the marking of projects. A substantial project may be marked against a number of criteria, and it is even more important than for an essay that people know what these criteria are before they start. For example, you might allocate marks as follows.

Presentation: 15 per cent
Information gathering: 20 per cent
Technical content: 30 per cent
Analysis: 20 per cent
Strength of proposals: 15 per cent

If possible, let people see examples of completed and successful projects before they start. Completing a project can be powerful learning exercise for someone. A project not only allows you to assess someone's competence, but also enables the learner to put much of what he or she has learned into practice. The project can help people outside the training function to see and appreciate the effects of the learning on performance.

Of course, some projects may not be written at all. A project could require a video film to be produced, an engine to be rebuilt or a house to be renovated. Again, care has to be taken to define the assessment criteria sufficiently to ensure as much objectivity as possible can be brought to bear.

FREE RESPONSE TESTS

Although essays and projects are very good for looking at some types of learning, they are never a complete examination of somebody's knowledge. When it is important to assess whether someone has achieved a thorough knowledge and understanding of technical subjects, tests can be more useful. A free response question is one which does not suggest an answer in any way, for example:

What is the capital of Denmark?

A variation on such a straightforward style of question is the structured question. A 'structured question' is one which has an initial, descriptive, introductory statement followed by successive subquestions which are designed to check comprehension or knowledge; for example:

An engineering company placed an advertisement for an electrician in a local newspaper. They received ten applications; nine from men and one from a woman. The company interviewed four of the men and appointed one of them. The woman decided to complain that she had been subject to discrimination.

(a) What is the most relevant piece of legislation covering this situation?
(b) How long would she have to register a complaint?
(c) Does the burden of proof lie with the company or the woman?
(d) What would be the maximum amount of compensation she might receive if successful?

(e) Give three arguments that the company might use in its defence against the allegation.

One of the important things to ensure when setting such a question is that you have a clear idea of what would constitute an acceptable or unacceptable answer. For example, would you require a date for part (a)? If so, would it not be fairer to amend the question to indicate this? Part (e) has some scope for the individual to select from a range of a possible arguments. Think through whether such a question would actually discriminate between people who understood the topic fully and those who were just good at guessing.

MULTIPLE CHOICE QUESTIONS

Multiple-choice item consists of a question or incomplete statement followed by a choice of answers, of which usually only one is correct; for example:

What is the capital of France:
   (a) Lyons
   (b) Marseilles
   (c) Paris
   (d) Poole
   (e) Rennes?

Variations on this format have been developed such as asking respondents to choose from a selection of combinations; for example:

The following are all locations in Europe:
Barcelona
Cognac
Rome
Oporto

Which of them does our company have offices in:
   (a) all of them
   (b) Barcelona, Cognac, and Rome
   (c) Barcelona, Cognac, and Oporto
   (d) Cognac, Rome and Oporto
   (e) Barcelona and Oporto only

    (f) Barcelona and Cognac only

    (g) Barcelona and Rome only

    (h) Cognac and Oporto only

    (i) Cognac and Rome only

    (j) Rome and Oporto only?

The first advantage of structuring the question in this way, rather than asking 'Which of the following does the company have an office in?' is that only one response is necessary, which simplifies marking. The second advantage is that the respondent is not confused into thinking that he or she has to choose only one of the options.

THE PERFORMANCE GRID

A concept developed by Stewart (1986) which can be useful for the evaluation of training is the performance grid. This provides an indirect measurement of performance which can be useful as a training need identification aid, but which becomes a strong assessment tool when used before and after training for people whose jobs are not easily measured by direct means.

The concept is based on the notion that two main components of current performance are motivation and skills. The individual's innate ability level is also important, but as that may be considered to be fixed, it may be disregarded for this purpose. Similarly, the opportunity to use skills may usually be ignored when comparing performance in a stable situation.

Managers or supervisors are asked to assess the two elements of performance separately for each person and place them in a performance grid (example 5.3).

The supervisor or manager is asked to identify the best and worst performer and to place each of them on the grid by reference to their motivation and skills level. A rating of 2 is at the 'best I've ever known' level, and 0 is at the 'worst I've ever known' level. This process is repeated – second best/second worst, and so on. Additional guidance may be given by the use of behavioural guidance anchors. An example is given below, but you might prefer

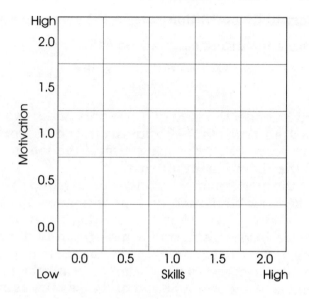

Example 5.3 Performance grid

to adapt the terms used in an existing system, such as a performance appraisal scheme.

Skills

0 Almost none of the skills or knowledge required in the job
0.5 Some skills and knowledge, but below the required standard
1 Skills and knowledge match the job requirements
1.5 Skills and knowledge exceed the job requirements
2 Skills and knowledge exceed the job requirements substantially

Motivation

0 No interest in the work whatsoever
0.5 Some interest in the work, shows concentration, but generally lacking in motivation
1 Averagely motivated
1.5 Above average motivation

2   Very high motivation

A performance rating can now be calculated:

$$PR = \frac{motivation + skills}{2}$$

For convenience, the sum of the scores of the two factors is halved so that staff who are assessed as competent have the score of 1 (they can perform the job to 100 per cent of the requirement for that job).

Once the performance ratings for a group are calculated, they can be plotted on a performance distribution graph (example 5.4). After the training programme, the ratings are made again, and a new graph is drawn. Any changes in the whole group's performance is now demonstrable. This method is particularly useful when a series of inputs is given over a period of time as the cumulative impact of the training is measured.

Giving Feedback

There are some situations when assessments are made without feedback, or with limited feedback. For example,

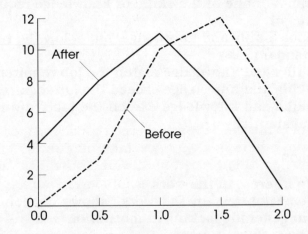

Example 5.4 Performance distribution graph

if you take an educational qualification examination you will probably be told only the grade that your efforts were assessed as being worth. In most training situations, you have to do more than this. You have to explain the reasons for giving the assessment that you did and what the learner must do to correct any deficiencies. This process requires tact and sensitivity. There are two outcomes to be particularly avoided.

- Telling someone that what they are doing is fine when in fact it is not
- Crushing them so that they do not wish to continue with the learning

I enjoy giving people praise and dislike criticizing them (to their faces, at least). Therefore I have to discipline myself when giving feedback to include 'points for improvement'. Incidentally, it does not matter what you call such feedback, some people will regard it as criticism. It is important to spend time diminishing this feeling by explaining the purpose of the feedback before the assessment event, and ensuring that certain rules are followed.

In technical training, feedback is often easily given in that there may be a definite right or wrong answer. In softer subjects a degree of subjectivity is present which can lead to differences of opinion and interpretation. Often more than one person can be involved in giving the feedback, and other learners' perceptions may be as good as or better than the trainer's.

Certain rules may apply to the giving of feedback:

- It should always be remembered that giving feedback in front of others is a very special situation. People have a right to their individuality and integrity, and the opportunity to give feedback is not a licence to have a go at someone.
- Offer feedback on what has been observed and try not to read motives into someone's behaviour which might not really be there. Say: 'I noticed that you avoided eye

contact with the interviewee' rather than 'You seemed to be scared of the interviewee'.

- Try to avoid being judgmental. Terms such as 'poor' or 'bad', or phrases like 'you shouldn't have' will make you sound like an old-fashioned schoolteacher. Instead, point out what was effective or ineffective. You can, however, say how you *felt*: 'I felt like I was being put on the spot when you chose me.'
- Focus on behaviour that can be changed. Telling someone that he tends to turn his back to the audience a lot may be useful; telling him that he would be more imposing if he were taller is not. Some feedback, even if valuable, needs to be given in private rather than in front of a group (e.g. comments about clothing or grooming).
- Do not overload people with things to work on or change. Concentrate on two or three key aspects for improvement. If someone is given a long list of areas which need improvement, he or she will feel demoralized and will not know where to start.
- Asking them what they thought of their own performance can be useful. It allows them a chance to acknowledge shortcomings for themselves, which may be more comfortable. You can also ask them why they did certain things and not others. Perhaps a learner will say that she chose to experiment to do things differently from how she normally does. This can then lead on to a useful discussion of the two approaches.
- In many feedback situations mistakes are okay. The whole point of the exercise is to learn from making mistakes. People also learn from observing others' mistakes. For this reason, those who go first are at a disadvantage, and later participants will have had the chance to avoid certain pitfalls. Bear this in mind if assessing performance.
- Comment on the things that were done well. Sometimes people are not aware of their own competence and need to be told. This helps to build confidence and sustain motivation.

One problem with verbal feedback is that it can be quickly forgotten. A useful idea when a video camera has been used to make a recording, perhaps of a presentation or an interview, is to leave the tape running to record the feedback as well. The learner can then play this back to himself or herself as required. Another option is to give written feedback. If you are making systematic assessments of a skilled performance, it makes sense to use the same format for feedback to the learner. It is also good practice to let people know what they will be assessed and given feedback on before they perform rather than afterwards. An example of a written assessment is given in example 5.5.

Psychometric Testing

Psychometric tests have long been used in the field of human resource management. However, this has been primarily to aid the process of selection for employment. They can, however, also be used for selection for training programmes. This can help to reduce the chances of people undertaking programmes that will be beyond their ability level. More recently, the publishers of tests have started to produce products which have application in the context of feedback about personal qualities at work which in turn can help to identify development needs. The same products can subsequently be used to measure whether changes have taken place.

HISTORY

The need for an objective measure of ability was first noted in the educational/clinical field. In France at the turn of the century, Binet developed tests to clarify which children were 'mentally defective'. The tests used were later developed into measures for use with adults. The concept of 'mental age' came into being. This was

Name:	
Assessment – instructional session	

Introduction		**Comments**
Introduced self	☐	
Introduced subject	☐	
Explained the need	☐	
Stated the range of the session	☐	
Stated the objective of the session	☐	
Put the learner at ease	☐	
Instruction		
Structure	☐	
Interaction with learner	☐	
Clarity of instructions	☐	
Answering questions	☐	
Checking understanding	☐	
Effectiveness	☐	
Time usage	☐	
Comments:		
Pass/Refer/Fail		

Example 5.5 Assessment sheet

compared with chronological age, and the term 'intelligence quotient' (IQ) was coined.

$$IQ = \frac{\text{Mental Age}}{\text{Chronological Age}} \times 100$$

By definition, therefore, average IQ is 100. This concept was useful in the clinical field. Over the years more tests were developed to measure IQ, among adults as well as children, and eventually the idea of doing this as an aid to selection for employment was born.

Nowadays, the idea of measuring IQ is considered not to be appropriate for selection because people differ in their abilities to function in a variety of mental areas, and a general IQ score can be misleading. Accordingly, modern tests used in non-clinical situations do not attempt to measure IQ, but instead measure aptitudes in clearly defined mental skills which are considered relevant to a particular job.

APTITUDE TESTS

Aptitude, or ability, tests measure performance in areas such as numerical reasoning, verbal reasoning or working with diagrams. They are usually targeted at a particular level of ability such as graduate level or apprentice level. They are usually easy to administer, score and interpret. They are used extensively for selection purposes. Because they are designed to measure ability as distinct from acquired knowledge they are not useful as an evaluation measure.

PERSONALITY QUESTIONNAIRES

Personality questionnaires attempt to analyse personality on the basis of the individual's answers to questions. These questions normally ask them to assess how they usually behave in certain situations, or what they would rather do when they have a choice, or how they consider themselves to be; for example: '*I consider myself to worry less than average*. True/False?'

The questionnaires available vary considerably in style and in the underlying theoretical concepts about personality that they are based on. They may be difficult to score and interpret, and require some skill to give feedback to people without upsetting them. Whether they are very useful in the training context is a matter of opinion. There are some aspects of personality that can be considered to be fundamental to us and impossible to change. Other aspects do change with time and experience. For example, you may have known someone who was once fairly shy and lacking in confidence but who got a job which, over time, transformed him or her into a more outgoing and confident person. These effects do not happen rapidly, and personality questionnaires may not always be an appropriate way of measuring such changes. None the less, they can give information on the effectiveness or otherwise of long-term development programmes, particularly those concerned with interpersonal skills, assertive behaviour and stress management.

Personality questionnaires may also give information about whether someone is likely to enjoy working with detail or not, or will tolerate chaos well, or needs challenge in a job. Again, such information can be helpful in determining who should undergo training.

INTEREST INVENTORIES

These ask about career and lifestyle preferences. They are often used in career counselling, and nowadays in out-placement. They are usually easy to use. One readily available instrument is the Careers Orientation Inventory available in Schein (1990) and distributed by Pfeiffer and Company (see Appendix 1).

FEEDBACK INSTRUMENTS

In response to the trend to provide feedback to managers from the people that they work with, a number of companies have developed instruments designed to produce information which can be useful when comparing the individual's self-perception with that of colleagues, bosses or subordinates. This is sometimes referred to as 360-degree feedback. One such instrument is the Personal Feedback Questionnaire produced by Knight Chapman Psychological. This provides measurements of the following dimensions.

Managing relationships

- Leadership
- Team membership
- Influencing
- Interpersonal awareness
- Development of others

Managing self

- Results orientation
- Energy and determination
- Resilicncc
- Structure
- Flexibility.

Managing operations

- Strategic awareness
- Creativity
- Problem solving
- Decision making
- Change management

An extract from a sample report is given in Appendix 2.

AVAILABILITY

For many years access to tests has been controlled to ensure that:

- tests do not circulate freely and thereby lose their validity as people practise and rehearse them

- consistent usage is assured, and standards do not vary from one administration to the next
- damage that can be caused by misuse is avoided
- test developers can be sure of recouping their outlay because photocopying and plagiarism is discouraged

All test providers have a registration system. In recent years the British Psychological Society has developed a generic system to standardize the approach to this, but some publishers still insist that you train with them to be able to buy their products. The British Psychological Society scheme is as follows.

Level A Available after a five-day course which gives access to most ability tests.

Level B Follows on from level A. A further five days plus one follow-up day (intermediate level) or two follow-up days (full). Level B gives access to a specific personality test (intermediate level) or to a wide range (full).

A list of test publishers is given in Appendix 3

'COWBOYS'

There are some publishers whose standards are much lower than required by the British Psychological Society. They sell personality tests of doubtful validity on the basis of a one-day course. Their sales personnel usually do not have a grounding in either psychology or human resources.

Summary

This chapter has looked at the related areas of evaluation, assessment and giving feedback. These are all important aspects of the role of the trainer which have been given increasing prominence in recent years.

Problems in the process of evaluation have been discussed, and a variety of evaluation methods have been explored. In particular, Kirkpatrick's system has been outlined and a simple approach to cost–benefit analysis given.

A number of approaches to assessment have also been considered, from straightforward criterion-referenced approaches through less direct methods such as essay writing to very indirect approaches such as the performance grid. It is hoped that most evaluation and assessment situations can be tackled using one or more of these methodologies.

The art of giving feedback has also been outlined. Whilst in many ways this topic could have been included in the section on delivery skills (chapter 4), the feedback process has an inherent element of assessment. In essence, feedback is a method of communicating assessments, however informally this is done.

Finally, a brief look at psychometric testing has been included with discussion about how that testing can be applied in a training context.

ACTIVITIES

1 Evaluation exercise A

Introduction This is an evaluation process design exercise that can be used as a follow-up activity to the programme design exercise given in chapter 2.

Aims To allow practice in the application of evaluation principles and discussion of issues arising.

Method Divide the class into small groups. Ask them to examine an existing training programme for which there is no real evaluation system in existence. Their task is to produce an evaluation plan showing how evaluation would be carried out at each of Kirkpatrick's four levels. This can then be presented to the whole class and discussed. An alternative is to use the programme design produced in accordance with the instructions in exercise 3 at the end of chapter 2.

It will be necessary to clarify and agree the degree of detail required in the plan. Decide whether 'a multiple choice test' is an adequate description or whether 'a multiple choice test consisting of 20 questions will be devised covering the following areas . . .' is required.

Timing Depending on the degree of detail required, between 45 minutes and two hours.

2 Evaluation exercise B

Introduction This is a detailed evaluation design exercise that can be used as a follow-up activity to the evaluation design exercise given above.

Aims To allow practice in the application of detailed evaluation techniques and discussion of issues arising.

Method Divide the class into small groups. Ask them to produce a finished test as proposed in the previous exercise. This can then be presented to the whole class and discussed. An alternative is to ask for a customized reaction evaluation form to be produced.

Timing Depending on the complexity of the task, between 30 minutes and one hour

3 Feedback demonstration

Introduction A short but memorable way to put across the importance of giving informative feedback.

Aims To stress the importance of giving as much information as possible to improve performance.

Method The group is divided into pairs, seated at tables.

Each pair is equipped with a pencil, paper and ruler. One person from each pair is then blindfolded. The blindfolded person is asked to draw a line exactly 10 centimetres in length. They are allowed ten attempts. After each attempt, the other person measures the line and announces 'right' or 'wrong' to the blindfolded person. To be right the line must be within 2 millimetres of the required 10 centimetres length.

After ten attempts, the rules for feedback change. The person giving feedback may now tell the blindfolded person exactly how long or short the line is. After ten further attempts the blindfolds are removed and the two sets of lines compared.

Timing   About 20 minutes.

4   Giving feedback exercise

Introduction   This is a simple exercise but it has the potential to cause some distress and so needs to be handled with care.

Aims   To give practice in the giving of feedback.

Method   The class is split into two groups. Group one sits in a circle and discusses a topic which may be given to them or chosen by them. This lasts for 20 minutes. Each of the people in the other half of the group is assigned the responsibility of observing one particular individual in the discussion. At the end of the 20 minutes, each participant is paired up with his or her observer who then gives feedback to him or her about how he or she behaved in the group discussion. The observers now form the discussion group, with the previous participants observing. It may be better not to have the same people paired as previously.

Variations

- The participant may be asked not to respond or comment during the feedback.
- The participant may be asked to give his or her reaction to the observer about the quality of the feedback given.
- The group may be divided into three. The third person's role is to observe the feedback process and then give feedback (in turn) as to the quality of the process.
- You may introduce rules about whether or not to have an even number of positive and negative observations, no negative observations, and so on.

Timing Depending on the way the exercise is structured, about an hour.

FURTHER READING

Garbutt, D. 1969: *Training Costs*. London: Gee.

Harrison, R. 1992: *Employee Development*. London: Institute of Personnel Management

Jackson, T. 1989: *Evaluation: Relating Training to Business Performance* London: Kogan Page.

Kirkpatrick, D. L. 1976: Evaluation of training. In R. L. Craig and L. R. Bittel (eds): *Training and Development Handbook*, New York: ASTO/McGraw-Hill.

Rae, L. 1995: *Techniques of Training* (3rd edn). Aldershot: Gower.

Reid, M. A., Barrington, H. and Kenney, J. 1992: *Training Interventions* (3rd edn). London: Institute of Personnel Management.

Sanderson, G. 1995: Objectives and evaluation. In Truelove, S. (ed.), *The Handbook of Training and Development*. Oxford: Blackwell.

Schein, E. H. 1990: *Career Anchors: Discovering Your Real Values*. San Diego: Pfeiffer.

Stewart, D. 1986: *The Power of People Skills*, New York: John Wiley.

Appendix 1   Useful Contacts

Investors in people

Investors in People UK
4th Floor
7–10 Chandos Street
London
W1M 9DE
Tel: 0171 467 1900

Investors in People (Scotland)
1 Washington Court
Washington Lane
Edinburgh
EH11 2HA
0131 346 1212

The Training and Employment Agency
Business Support Division
Clarendon House
9–21 Adelaide Street
Belfast
BT2 8DJ
Tel: 01232 541732

Books and videos

(B) = books, (V) = videos

Academy Television
(V)
104 Kirkstall Road
Leeds
LS3 1JS
Tel: 0113 246 1528

Connaught Training Ltd
(B+V)
Gower House
Croft Road
Aldershot
Hampshire
GU11 3HR
Tel: 01252 331551

Flex Training Ltd
(B+V)
9–15 Hitchin Street
Baldock
Herts
SG7 6AL
Tel: 01462 895544

Guild Sound and Vision Ltd
(V)
6 Royce Road
Peterborough
PE1 5YB
Tel: 01733 315315

Jumpcut
(V)
Bank Chambers

2 Lidget Hill
Pudsey
West Yorkshire
LS28 7DP
Tel: 0113 256 6544

Industrial Society
(B+V)
National Sales Unit
Quadrant Court
49 Calthorpe Road
Edgbaston
Birmingham
B15 1TH
Tel: 0121 454 6769

Institute of Personnel and Development
(B)
Publishing Department
IPD House
35 Camp Road
Wimbledon
London
SW19 4UX
Tel: 0181 263 3387

Kantola Productions
(V)
c/o Conference Support International
The Old Granary
27–29 Chester Road
Castle Bromwich
Birmingham
B36 9DA
Tel: 0121 776 7799

Melrose Film Productions Ltd
(B+V)
16 Bromells Road

London
SW4 0BL
Tel: 0171 627 8404

National Council for Vocational Qualifications
(B)
222 Euston Road
London NW1 2EZ
Tel: 0171 387 9898

Pfeiffer and Company
(B+V)
27 Harborough Business Park
Lodge Road
Long Harborough
Witney
Oxfordshire
OX8 8LH
Tel: 01993 883994

Video Arts Ltd
(V)
Dumbarton House
68 Oxford Street
London
W1N 9LA
Tel: 0171 637 7288

Appendix 2 Extract From the Report From a 360-Degree Feedback Instrument

(Reproduced with the kind permission of Andrew Roberts of Knight Chapman Psychological Limited.)

The Personal Feedback Questionnaire

Your hierarchy versus others' perceptions

Following is based on the *average* score given to you by your colleagues.

Your hierarchy	*Their hierarchy*
Flexibility	Resilience
Customer focus	Customer focus
Strategic thinking	Flexibility
Decision making	Self awareness
Teamwork	Developing others
Developing others	Influence
Structure	Awareness of change
Resilience	Analytical thinking
Awareness of change	Strategic thinking
Analytical thinking	Teamwork
Self awareness	Decision making
Business planning	Creativity

Creativity	Business planning
Leadership	Leadership
Influence	Structure

Key points There are some close relationships between perceived areas of strength and areas for improvement in these hierarchies.

Flexibility and Customer focus feature quite highly. Business planning, Leadership and Creativity equally figure as areas for improvement.

The greatest areas of mismatch are Influence where others rate you much more highly than you rate yourself; Resilience, where again others give you higher ratings than you do; Decision making, where your self perception is stronger than that of others; and to a lesser extent, Strategic thinking where your view is generally somewhat higher than that of your colleagues.

Appendix 3   Psychometric Test Distributors

(Note: this is not a comprehensive list.)

ASE
Darville House
2 Oxford Road East
Windsor
Berkshire
SL4 1DF
Tel: 01753 861777

Knight Chapman Psychological Ltd
48 High Street
Lewes
Sussex
BN7 2DD
Tel: 01273 4872333

Oxford Psychologists Press Ltd
311–321 Banbury Road
Oxford
OX2 7JH
Tel: 01865 510203

Psytech International Ltd
Icknield House
Eastcheap

Letchworth
Hertfordshire
SG6 3DA
Tel: 01462 482833

The Psychological Corporation Ltd
24–28 Oval Road
London
NW1 7DX
Tel: 0171 267 4466

Saville and Holdsworth Ltd
3 AC Court
High Street
Thames Ditton
Surrey
KT7 0SR
Tel: 0181 398 4170

Index